A-Z EASTE

CONTENT

Key to Map Pages	Back Cover
Large Scale Pages	2-3
Map Pages	4-23

Index
Villag
& sele... Places of Interest

REFERENCE

A Road	A259
B Road	B2191
Dual Carriageway	
One-way Street Traffic flow on A Roads is also indicated by a heavy line on the driver's left.	
Road Under Construction Opening dates are correct at the time of publication	
Proposed Road	
Restricted Access	
Pedestrianized Road	
Track / Footpath	
Residential Walkway	
Railway	Station, Level Crossing, Tunnel
Built-up Area	CHURCH ST.
Local Authority Boundary	
National Park Boundary	
Posttown Boundary	
Postcode Boundary (within Posttown)	
Map Continuation	14 / Large Scale Town Centre 2
Car Park (selected)	P
Church or Chapel	†
Cycle Route (selected)	
Fire Station	■
Hospital	H
House Numbers (A & B Roads only)	10 24
Information Centre	i
National Grid Reference	560
Police Station	▲
Post Office	★
Safety Camera with Speed Limit Fixed cameras and long term road works cameras. Symbols do not indicate camera direction.	30
Toilet: without facilities for the Disabled with facilities for the Disabled for exclusive use by the Disabled	▽
Viewpoint	
Educational Establishment	
Hospital or Healthcare Building	
Industrial Building	
Leisure or Recreational Facility	
Place of Interest	
Public Building	
Shopping Centre or Market	
Other Selected Buildings	

SCALE

Map Pages 4-23
1:15,840 4 inches (10.16 cm) to 1 mile 6.31 cm to 1km
0 ¼ ½ Mile
0 250 500 750 Metres

Map Pages 2-3
1:7,920 8 inches (20.32 cm) to 1 mile 12.63 cm to 1km
0 ⅛ ¼ Mile
0 100 200 300 Metres

Fairfield Road, Borough Green, Sevenoaks, Kent TN15 8PP
Telephone: 01732 781000 (Enquiries & Trade Sales)
01732 783422 (Retail Sales)

www.az.co.uk

Edition 5 2012

2
Old Town
HIGH ST. THE
UPPERTON
A2270
A259
GOFFS
Eastbourne
Gildredge Park
Manor Gardens
Royal Eastbourne Golf Course
Compton Place
Compton Park
The Saffrons (Cricket & Football Ground)
BN20
Meads
University of Brighton (Welkin Site)
University of Brighton (Hillbrow Site)
Trevin Towers
Eastbourne County & Magistrates' Court
Town Hall
Library
Grange Gardens
Gonville House (Eastbourne College)
Eastbourne College
Hartfield Square
Upperton Gdns.
THE AVENUE
A2040
ROAD
Sports Ground
Temple Grove
Club House
Superstore
Playing Field
19
23
98
99
560
A
B
C
D
1
2
3
4
5
6

EASTBOURNE
ENGLISH CHANNEL
Pier
Camera Obscura
Landing Stages
Bandstand
The Carpet Gds.
Allchorn Pleasure Boats
The Wish Tower
(Martello Tower no.73)
Western Lawns
Lifeboat Mus.
Devonshire Park
Devonshire Park Theatre
Winter Garden
Congress Theatre
Theatre Heritage Cen.
Museum
ESPERANCE HOSP
Musgrave Museum
Royal Hippodrome Theatre
Curzon Cin.
Club
Synagogue
ARNDALE CENTRE
Sussex Gdns
Bourne Primary School
Mosque
Depot
TA Centre
YMCA
GRAND PARADE
MARINE PARADE
ROYAL PARADE
SEASIDE
SEASIDE RD.
TERMINUS RD.
TRINITY TREES
DEVONSHIRE PLACE
SUSAN'S ROAD
ASHFORD ROAD
CAVENDISH PLACE
KING EDWARDS PARADE
A259
B2103
B2106
BN21
BN22
E
F
G
H
1
2
3
4
5
6
20
3
099
98
62

A
B
C
D
1
2
3
4
5
6
57
58
13
12
11
110
TN21
Well Shaw
Hopgarden Shaw
Leabridge Farm
Boggy Wood
Parsonage Barn
THE GRANARY RURAL BUS. CEN.
Broad Farm
Lea Bridge
Hill Harbour
Stone House Farm
VICARAGE
CHURCH LA.
LANE
MILL
CHURCH PTH.
The Vicarage
Cuckmere
River
Trail
Nursery
HELLINGLY
Hall
CHURCH
Hellingly Primary School
STATION ROAD
Horselunges
Station House
Moat
ROAD
Cemy.
War Mem.
NORTH STREET
A267
B2104
Woods Corner
White House
Lower Horsebridge
Hailsham
BN27
Cuckoo
Nursery
Longfields
A271
UPPER HORSEBRIDGE ROAD
P
Pav.
Rec. Grd.
Bowl. Grn.
Brook House
Knights Farm
THE A22 DICKER
BOSHIP RBT.
NEW
Factory
Hotel
Horse Bridge
Mill
THE WILLOWS
BAKERS FARM PARK HOMES
Upper Horsebridge
Horselunges Wood
Upper Horselunges Farm
Mill Bri.
LONDON ROAD
MANOR PARK CL.
MANOR PARK ROAD
LANSDOWNE
Prim. Sch.
Play. Fid.
SOLENT CRES.
LUNDY WLK.
ANGLESEY AV.
ROCKALL DR.
THE PADDOCKS
ASHBURNHAM PL.
STROMA GDNS.
SOLWAY
ARRAN CL.
MEDWAY
FAIRISLE CL.
MORAY WK.
BRUNEL DR.
BRUNEL DRIVE
HEDLEY WAY
GOODWIN CL.
CROMER
AVENUE
LEAP CROSS SMALL BUS. CEN.
HAWKSWOOD
DOUGLAS CL.
BEXLEY CL.
HAWTHYLANDS
MILLAND RD.
FERN GRN.
JASMINE GRN.
BLOSSOM
OLDFIELD CR.
ILEX GR.
MILLAND
Air Strip
River
Cuckmere
HEMPSTEAD LANE
Woodside Farm
GLENEAGLES
GREENFIELDS
Hempstead Farm
Chicheley Farm (Caravan Site)
Tile Hurst
A22
Grovelands Prim. Sch.
Resource Cen.
WOBURN CL.
DUNBAR DR.
DERWENT CL.
GROVELANDS RD.
LAVENDER CL.
PITREAVIE DR.
Grovelands Farm
CAMERON
Playing Fi
Ten. Cts.
Hailsham Comm. Coll.
THE CEDARS
Tilehurst
Tile Hurst
6

4
TN21
Well Shaw
Hopgarden Shaw
Leabridge Farm
Lea Bridge
Hill Harbour
Boggy Wood
Parsonage Barn
THE GRANARY RURAL BUS. CEN.
Broad Farm
Stone House Farm
NORTH STREET
A267
VICARAGE LANE
CHURCH LA.
MILL LANE
River Cuckmere
The Vicarage
HELLINGLY
STATION ROAD
Hall
Hellingly Primary School
Horselunges
Station House
Moat
Cemy.
War Mem.
B2104
Nursery
Hailsham
BN27
Woods Corner
White House
Lower Horsebridge
Cuckoo Trail
Longfields
Horselunges Wood
Upper Horselunges Farm
A271
Brook House
Knights Farm
Rec. Grd.
Bowl. Grn.
Horse Bridge
Mill
Upper Horsebridge
THE WILLOWS
BAKERS FARM PARK HOMES
UPPER HORSEBRIDGE ROAD
THE DICKER
A22
BOSHIP RBT.
Factory
Hotel
Mill Bri.
LONDON ROAD
MANOR PARK RD.
LANSDOWNE DRIVE
Prim. Sch.
Play. Fld.
HAWKS ROAD
HAWTHYLANDS
Air Strip
River Cuckmere
BRUNEL DR.
HEDLEY WAY
HEMPSTEAD LANE
GLENEAGLES
Woodside Farm
Hempstead Farm
Chicheley Farm (Caravan Site)
Tile Hurst
Grovelands Prim. Sch.
Resource Cen.
MILLAND RD.
Playing Fields
Ten. Cts.
Hailsham Comm. Coll.
GROVELANDS RD.
CAMERON
Grovelands Farm
Tilehurst
Tile Hurst
6

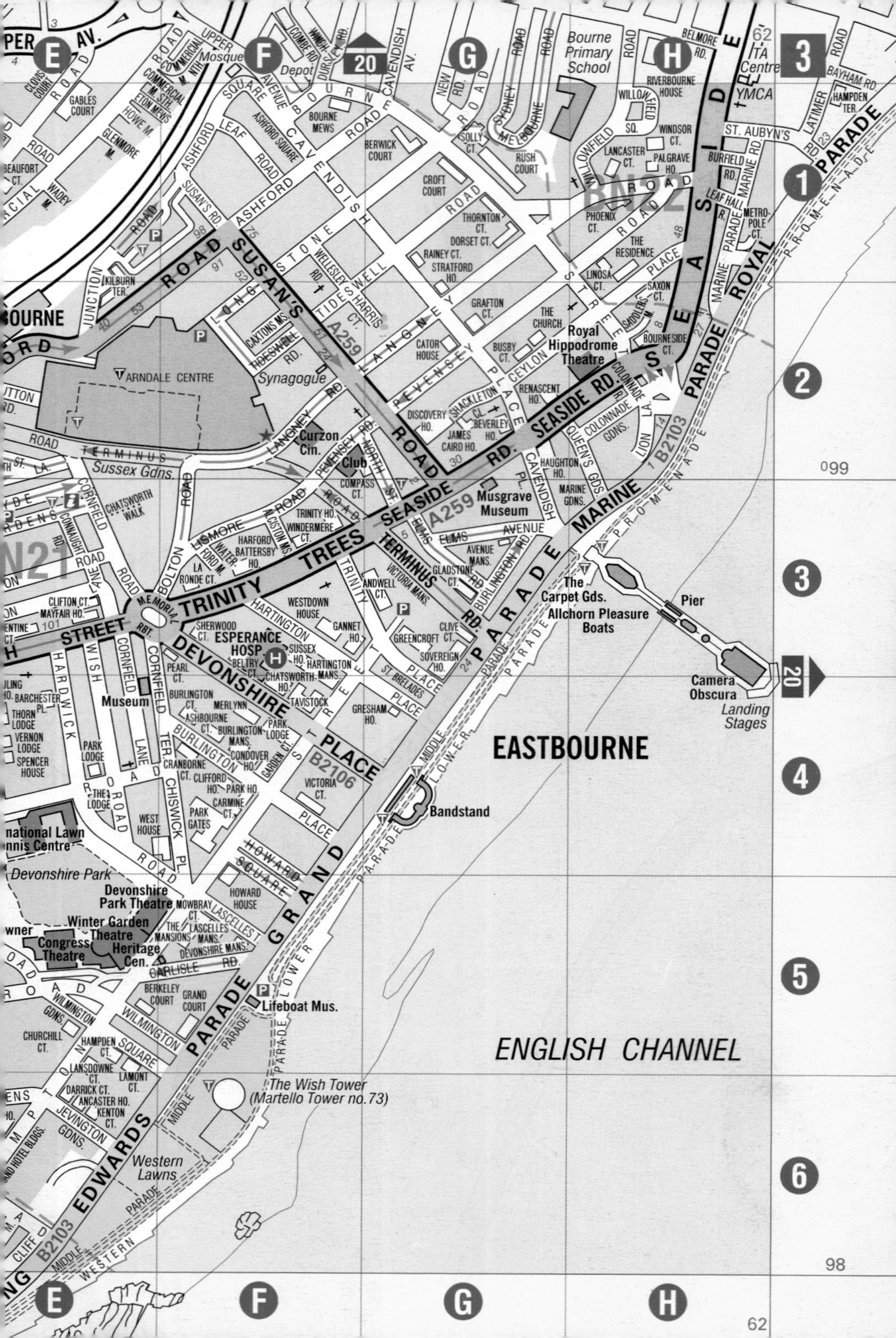

E
F
G
H
20
3
1
2
3
4
5
6
099
98
Bourne Primary School
Mosque
Depot
TA Centre
YMCA
BN22
BN21
ARNDALE CENTRE
Synagogue
Curzon Cin.
Club
Musgrave Museum
Royal Hippodrome Theatre
Museum
ESPERANCE HOSP.
Sussex Gdns.
MEMORIAL RBT.
TRINITY TREES
SEASIDE
SEASIDE RD.
SUSAN'S ROAD
TERMINUS
DEVONSHIRE PLACE
GRAND PARADE
MARINE PARADE
ROYAL PARADE
KING EDWARDS PARADE
A259
B2103
B2106
The Carpet Gds.
Allchorn Pleasure Boats
Pier
Camera Obscura
Landing Stages
EASTBOURNE
Bandstand
ENGLISH CHANNEL
National Lawn Tennis Centre
Devonshire Park
Devonshire Park Theatre
Winter Garden
Congress Theatre
Theatre Heritage Cen.
Lifeboat Mus.
The Wish Tower (Martello Tower no.73)
Western Lawns

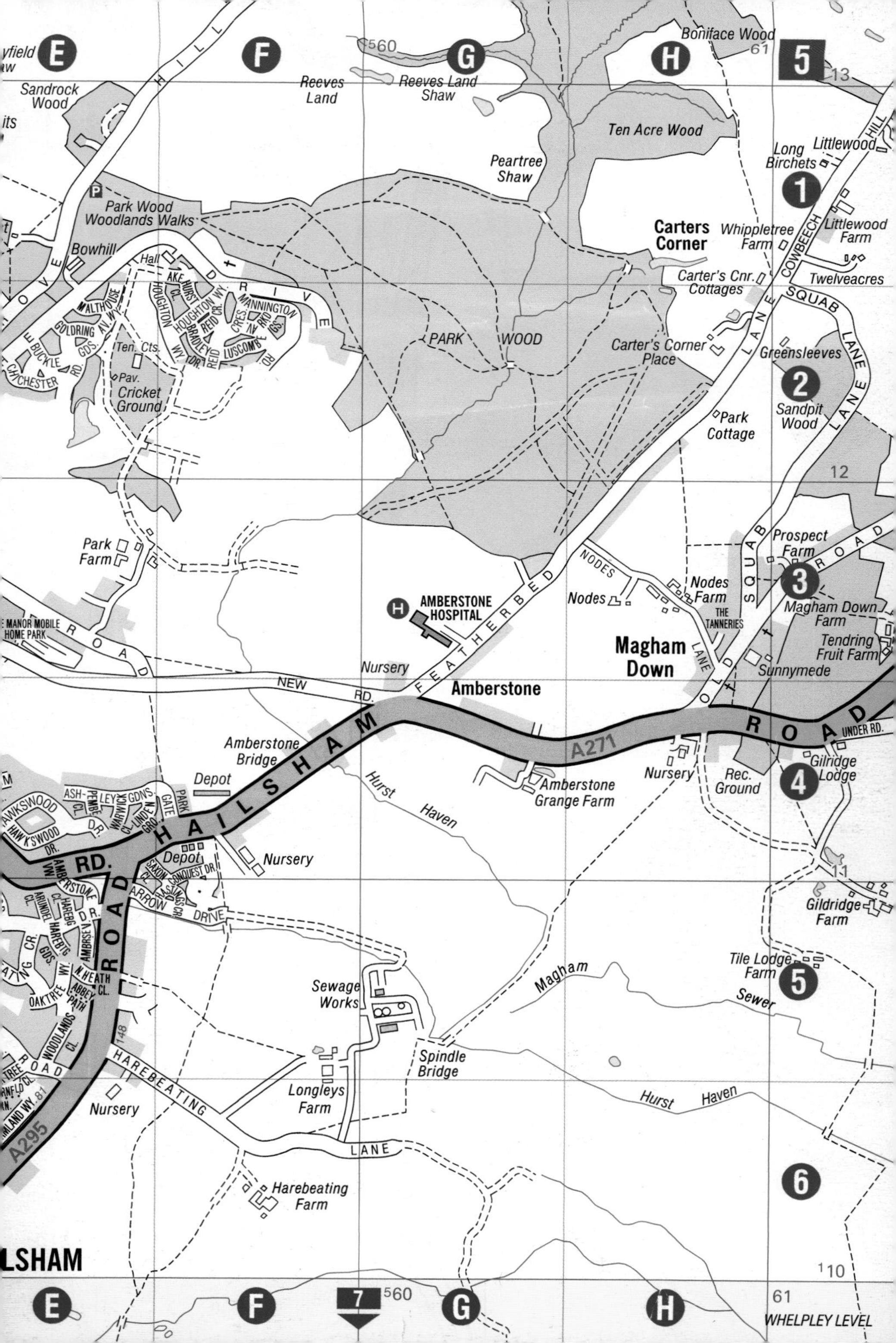
5
E
F
G
H
Sandrock Wood
Reeves Land
Reeves Land Shaw
Boniface Wood
Ten Acre Wood
Peartree Shaw
Park Wood Woodlands Walks
Bowhill
Carters Corner
Long Birchets
Littlewood
Whippletree Farm
Littlewood Farm
Twelveacres
Carter's Cnr. Cottages
Carter's Corner Place
Greensleeves
Sandpit Wood
Park Cottage
PARK WOOD
Cricket Ground
Park Farm
Prospect Farm
Nodes Farm
Nodes
AMBERSTONE HOSPITAL
Magham Down Farm
Tendring Fruit Farm
Magham Down
Sunnymede
Nursery
Amberstone
NEW RD.
FEATHERBED LANE
SQUAB LANE
COWBEECH HILL
HAILSHAM ROAD
A271
UNDER RD.
Gilridge Lodge
Amberstone Bridge
Depot
Amberstone Grange Farm
Rec. Ground
Hurst Haven
Gildridge Farm
Tile Lodge Farm
Magham Sewer
Sewage Works
Spindle Bridge
Longleys Farm
HAREBEATING LANE
Harebeating Farm
A295
HAILSHAM
7
WHELPLEY LEVEL

6
A
B
C
D
4
8
1
2
3
4
5
6
Chicheley Farm (Caravan Site)
Tile Hurst
Tilehurst Farm
Knock Hatch Cottage
Falconry Centre
Knock Hatch Farm
Knockhatch Adventure Park
Dry Ski Slope
Ruffet's Wood
Hidgate Cott.
Arlington Stadium (Speedway)
Highlands Farm Cottages
Highlands Farm
Bushy Wood (Scout Camp)
Bushy Wood Farm
Robin Post
Highlands Wood
WILMINGTON WOOD
Gillridge Wood
Robin Post Wood
ARLINGTON EAGLES ROUNDABOUT
Bolney's Farm
Bolney's Wood
Coldthorn Wood
Folkington Wood
Woodside Hall
Tudor Close
Summer Hill
Gate Wood
Natewood Farm
Brownings
Depot
Coppards
BN26
Woodside Poultry Farm
Cliff Coombe
Nightingale Place
Oaklands
Ersham House
Cemetery
Ersham Farm
Recreation Ground
Hailsham Comm. Coll.
Grovelands Farm
Diplocks Farm
HAILSHAM INDUSTRIAL PK.
NORTH CRESCENT IND.EST.
BURFIELD PARK INDUSTRIAL ESTATE
APEX PARK
Resource Cen.
Prim. Sch.
Playing Fields
Mulbrook Farm
PEEL HOUSE FARM CARAVAN PARK
A22
A295
B2104
HEMPSTEAD LANE
ARLINGTON ROAD WEST
ARLINGTON ROAD EAST
DIPLOCKS WAY
SOUTH RD.
POLEGATE RD.
LONDON ROAD
SUMMERHEATH RD.
WESTERN RD.
ERSHAM RD.
ERSHAM LANE
COLDTHORN LANE
HILL
SUMMER HILL
ROBIN POST LANE
WOODSIDE WAY
ROBIN
NATE WOOD

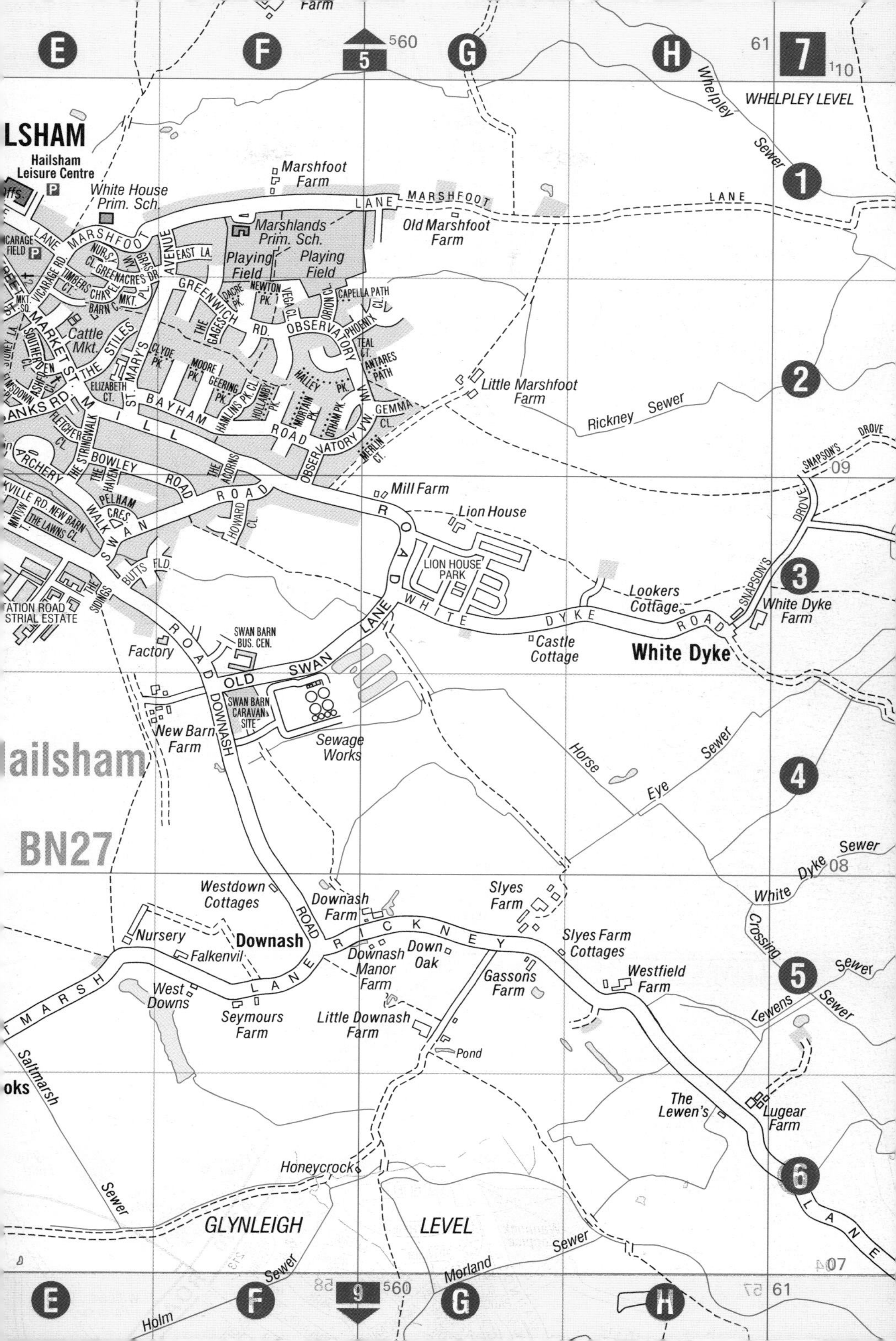

7
5
9
E
F
G
H
1
2
3
4
5
6
560
61
110
09
08
07
WHELPLEY LEVEL
Whelpley Sewer
LSHAM
Hailsham Leisure Centre
White House Prim. Sch.
Marshfoot Farm
MARSHFOOT LANE
Old Marshfoot Farm
Marshlands Prim. Sch.
Playing Field
Playing Field
EAST LA.
AVENUE
GREENWICH RD.
OBSERVATORY
CAPELLA PATH
NEWTON PK.
VEGA CL.
ORION CL.
PHOENIX
TEAL CT.
ANTARES PATH
HALLEY PK.
MORTAIN PK.
OTHAM PK.
GEMMA CL.
OBSERVATORY VW.
MERLIN CT.
Cattle Mkt.
MARKET ST.
VICARAGE RD.
THE STILES
ST. MARY'S
CLYDE PK.
MOORE PK.
GEERING PK.
HAMLINS PK. CL.
HOLLAMBY PK.
BAYHAM ROAD
MILL ROAD
ELIZABETH CT.
BANKS RD.
THE STRINGWALK
FLETCHER CL.
BOWLEY ROAD
THE HAVEN
THE ACORNS
ARCHERY
PELHAM CRES.
WALK
SWAN ROAD
HOWARD CL.
NEW BARN CL.
THE LAWNS
BUTTS FLD.
THE SIDINGS
STATION ROAD INDUSTRIAL ESTATE
Little Marshfoot Farm
Rickney Sewer
SNAPSON'S DROVE
Mill Farm
Lion House
LION HOUSE PARK
ROAD
WHITE DYKE ROAD
Lookers Cottage
White Dyke Farm
Castle Cottage
White Dyke
SWAN BARN BUS. CEN.
Factory
OLD SWAN LANE
SWAN BARN CARAVAN SITE
Sewage Works
New Barn Farm
DOWNASH ROAD
Hailsham
BN27
Horse Eye Sewer
White Dyke Sewer
Crossing
Westdown Cottages
Downash Farm
Slyes Farm
Nursery
Downash
Falkenvil
RICKNEY LANE
Downash Manor Farm
Down Oak
Slyes Farm Cottages
Gassons Farm
Westfield Farm
Lewens Sewer
SALTMARSH
West Downs
Seymours Farm
Little Downash Farm
Pond
Saltmarsh Sewer
The Lewen's
Lugear Farm
Honeycrock
GLYNLEIGH LEVEL
Sewer
Morland
Holm Sewer
LANE

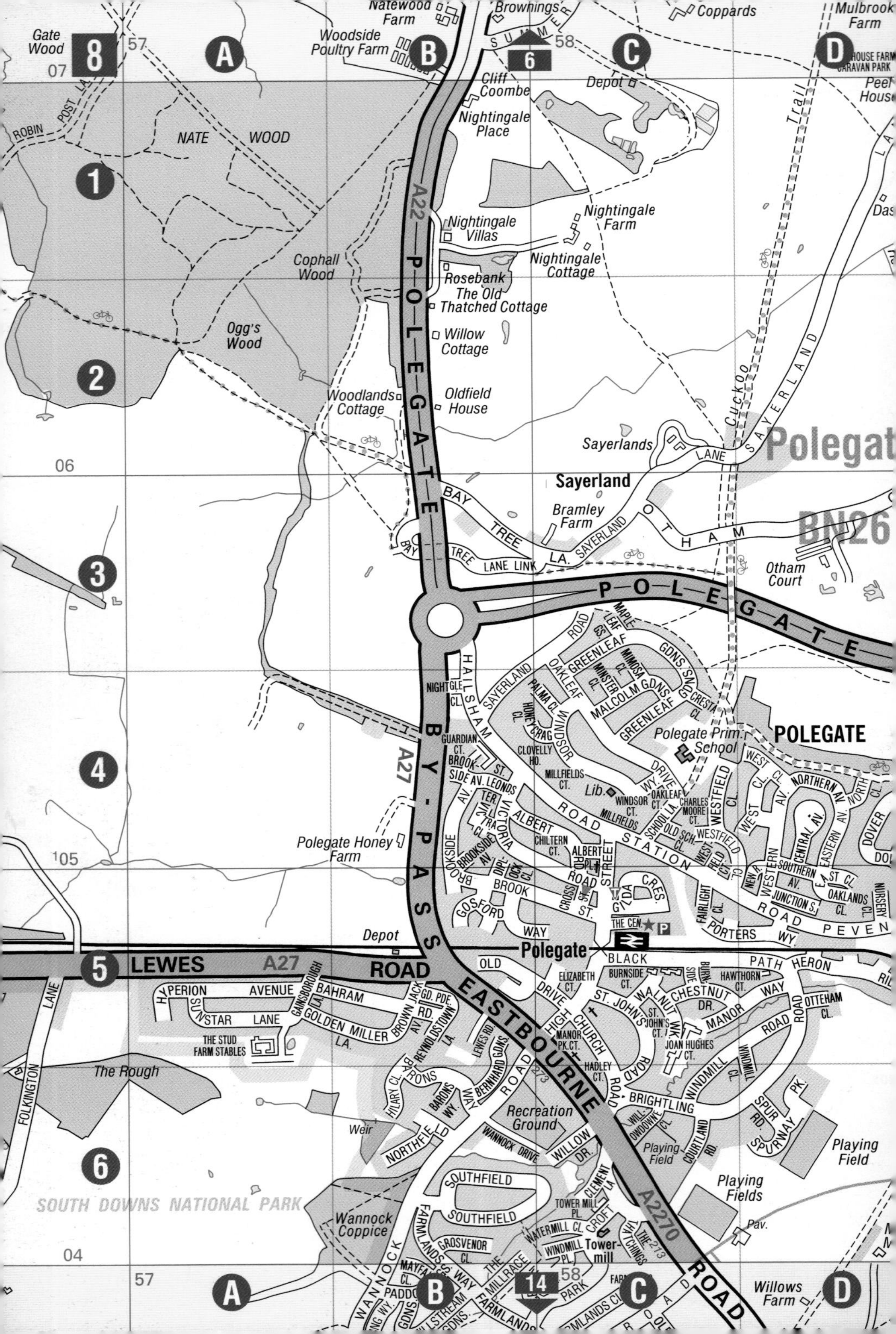

8
6
14
A
B
C
D
1
2
3
4
5
6
Gate Wood
Natewood Farm
Woodside Poultry Farm
Brownings
Coppards
Mulbrook Farm
Cliff Coombe
Depot
Peel House
NATE WOOD
Nightingale Place
ROBIN POST LA.
A22
POLEGATE
Nightingale Villas
Nightingale Farm
Cophall Wood
Nightingale Cottage
Rosebank
The Old Thatched Cottage
Willow Cottage
Ogg's Wood
Woodlands Cottage
Oldfield House
Sayerlands
Polegate
Sayerland
Bramley Farm
BN26
Otham Court
CUCKOO
Trail
SAYERLAND LANE
OTHAM
BAY TREE LA.
BAY TREE LANE LINK
POLEGATE
A27
BY-PASS
HAILSHAM ROAD
Polegate Prim. School
POLEGATE
Lib.
Polegate Honey Farm
STATION ROAD
Depot
Polegate
LEWES ROAD
A27
EASTBOURNE ROAD
A2270
HYPERION AVENUE
SUNSTAR LANE
BAHRAM
GOLDEN MILLER LA.
THE STUD FARM STABLES
FOLKINGTON LANE
The Rough
Weir
SOUTH DOWNS NATIONAL PARK
Wannock Coppice
Recreation Ground
Playing Field
Playing Fields
Tower-mill
Willows Farm
SOUTHFIELD
WANNOCK
FARMLANDS

E
F
G
H
7
560
61
9
07
BN27
Glynleigh Sewer
Sewer
Holm
GLYNLEIGH LEVEL
Holmmarsh Bridge
B2104
Morland
Glynleigh Farm
Boat House
Glyndley Manor (Hotel)
GLYNDLEY MANOR COTTAGE ESTATE
Warren Plantation
Heatherdene
Drockmill
Decoy Wood
East Lodge
ROAD
Marland Bridge
Marland
West Lodge
LANE
GLYNLEIGH
Pit (disused)
New Barn Farmhouse
New Barn Farm
Glynleigh Cottage
COTTAGE LA.
New Barn Cottage
HAILSHAM
Little Friars Farm
Old Court Cotts.
Priesthawes Farm
Sewer
LANE
Lower Priesthawes Cottages
06
Puddle
Priesthawes
Pevensey
Duck
SHEPHAM
BN24
Gut
Shepham Wood
Hill
A27
The Pines
10
Drockmill
B2104
Little Shepham
SHEPHAM LANE
BY-PASS
Sharnfold Cottages
CHURCH CL.
SHEPHAM LA.
GLYNLEIGH DR.
Sharnfold Farm
Greenacres
105
Ditton's Corner
LEVETT CL.
FAIROAKS
DROCK-MILL CL.
Blackness
ROAD
DITTONS
RUSSET CL.
BLEN-HEIM CL.
Depot
PEVENSEY
A27
BY - PASS
ROAD
ABERDALE
BRAMLEY RD.
MARY'S
ROAD
CHAUCER BUS. PK.
HOLLY ARCH CARAVAN SITE
Works
DITTONS
The Dell
Mill
CHAUCER INDUSTRIAL ESTATE
Dittons
B2247
BARN CL.
RED DYKE COTTAGES
ROAD
Ditch
GOLDEN
HAMBLE RD.
ARUN
Hankham Place
DARWELL DR.
HANKHAM CT.
MEDWAY
DARENT CL.
AV.
BEAULIEU
JUBILEE
STOUR CL.
CHERWELL CL.
KENNET WAY
Eastbourne
ROTHER
TILLINGHAM WY.
A22
LAMBOURN AV.
TILLINGHAM CL.
MOLE CL.
WELLSBOURNE
Willingdon & West Langney Sewer
BN22
SWALE CL.
04
Willingdon
15
560
WAY
61
BROAD OAK CL.
STONEGATE
LAUGHTON

A
B
C
D
1
2
3
4
5
6
Rickney Lane
New Bridge Rd.
Rickney Farm
Elmhurst
Road
Rickney
Bridge Farm
Sewer
Glynleigh
Gut
Hill
Drockmill
Decoy Wood
East Lodge
Glynleigh Road
Lusteds
Silverdale
Old Acre
Brown Cottage
Lusteds Cottage
Lusteds Farm
Horns Cross Farm
Windyridge
Rickney Street
Gurr Farm
Broadlands Farm
Hankham
Gut
Lower Priesthawes Cottages
Montague Wood
Montague
Wychehurst
Hankham Nurseries
Pevensey
BN24
Hankham
Hankham Primary School
HANKHAM
Jubilee Cottage Farm
Jenkins' Green
Hall
Hankham Cross
Hankham Street
Foords Lane
Street
Road
Poultry Farm
Saxon Nurseries
Hankham Hall Farm
Poultry Houses
Nursery
Hailsham
Sharnfold Cottages
Sharnfold Farm
Greenacres
Milton
Smallholdings
Peelings
B2104
Hankham
A27
Pevensey
Peelings Lane
Rattle
Blackness
The Dell
Dittons
Barn Cl.
St. Michaels Cl.
The Crossways
Pickens Wood
Peelings
Glessing Rd.
Banner Wy.
Boniface Cl.
Dallaway Dr.
Geering Rd.
Beechfield Cl.
STONE CROSS
Mill View Cl.
B2247
Road
Lion
Hamble Rd.
Arun
Darwell Dr.
Hankham Place
Medway La.
Hankham Ct.
Beaulieu Cl.
Adur Drive
Mimram Rd.
Prim. Sch.
Rattle
Windmill Grn.
Lane
Mill Crest
Nursery
Stone Cross Towermill
Uplands Farm
Darent Cl.
Av.
Kennet Wy.
Tillingham
Meon Cl.
Way
Orwell Cl.
Drive
Pride Vw.
Clayton Mill Rd.
Nutley Mill Rd.
Blatchington Dr.
Beggar's
Stour Cl.
Rother Cl.
Lambourn Av.
Tillingham Cl.
Mole Cl.
Tamar Cl.
Wellsbourne Rd.
Swale Cl.
Eden Cl.
Medina Dr.
Lavant Rd.
B2104
Hill
Patcham Mill
Bartley Mill
Shipley Mill Cl.
Singleton Mill Rd.
Friday St.
Rookery Farm Caravan Park
Boship
Hadlow
Michelham
Hodcombe Cl.
Pagham
Broad Oak Cl.
Laughton
Flimwell Cl.
Burwash Cl.
Whitbread Cl.
Borrowdale Cl.
16
9
61
62
07
06
105
104

11
Hailsham
BN27
Chilley Green
Chilley Farm
Chilley Bridge
Manxey Sewer
MANXEY LEVEL
Callow Stream
HANKHAM LEVEL
Martin's Ditch and Gut
Martin's Ditch
Churchlands Farm
LAPWING BUSINESS PARK
A27 BY-PASS
A259
MARSH ROAD
PEVENSEY RBT.
Pevensey Bri.
BRIDGE END
BEXHILL ROAD
12
SLUICE RD.
Bridge Farm
PEVENSEY
WESTHAM
Hankham Level
Castle Farm
HIGH ST.
CASTLE ROAD
B2191
WALLSEND RD.
Pevensey Castle & Anderida Roman Fort
Church Farm
Rec. Grd.
Fence Bridge
Anderita Park
Pevensey & Westham Prim. Sch.
Play. Fld.
Pevensey Bay
Works
Pevensey & Westham
PEVENSEY PARK ROAD
SPRINGFIELD CLOSE
Mount Pleasant
MONTAGUE WY.
CHURCH BAILEY WY.
EASTBOURNE RD.
PELHAM CL.
HOBNEY RISE
GREGORY LANE
FAIRFIELDS FARM CARAVAN PARK
Fairfields Farm
POTTS MARSH INDUSTRIAL ESTATE
WESTHAM BUS. PARK
MOUNTNEY BRI. BUSINESS PK.
17
MOUNTNEY LEVEL
Langney Sewer
New Mountney Sewer
Ditch
Mill
E
F
G
H
1
2
3
4
5
6

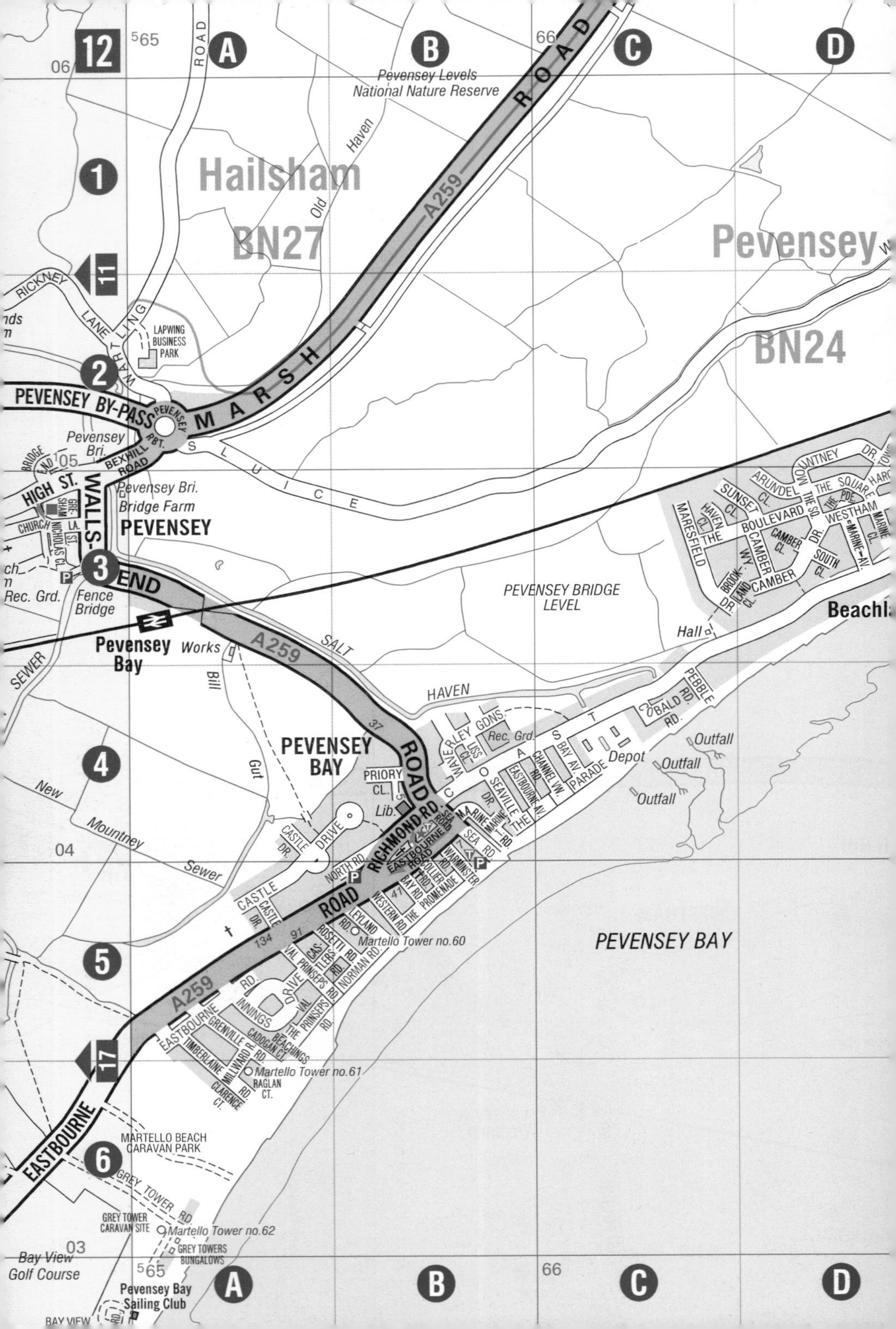
Pevensey Levels
National Nature Reserve
Hailsham
BN27
Pevensey
BN24
MARSH ROAD
A259
Old Haven
RICKNEY LANE
WARTLING ROAD
LAPWING BUSINESS PARK
PEVENSEY BY-PASS
PEVENSEY RBT.
SLUICE
BEXHILL ROAD
Pevensey Bri.
BRIDGE END
HIGH ST.
WALLS-END
CHURCH LA.
GRESHAM
NICHOLAS CL.
Pevensey Bri.
Bridge Farm
PEVENSEY
Rec. Grd.
Fence Bridge
Pevensey Bay
Works
SALT HAVEN
Bill Gut
PEVENSEY BRIDGE LEVEL
Hall
Beachl
MOUNTNEY DR.
ARUNDEL CL.
SUNSET CL.
HAVEN CL.
MARESFIELD
THE BOULEVARD
THE SQUARE
THE PDE.
WESTHAM DR.
MARINE AV.
MARINE CL.
CAMBER CL.
CAMBER WY.
CAMBER
SOUTH CL.
BROOKLAND CL.
DR.
PEBBLE RD.
THEOBALD RD.
COAST RD.
WAVERLEY GDNS.
LISS CL.
Rec. Grd.
BAY AV.
CHANNEL VW.
EASTBOURNE AV.
SEAVILLE DR.
PARADE
Depot
Outfall
Outfall
Outfall
PEVENSEY BAY
PRIORY CL.
Lib.
ROAD
RICHMOND RD.
MARINE RD.
SEA RD.
WARMINSTER RD.
CASTLE DR.
DRIVE
New Mountney Sewer
NORTH RD.
EASTBOURNE ROAD
COLLIER RD.
BAY RD.
PROMENADE
THE PROMENADE
WESTERN RD.
LEYLAND RD.
CASTLE DR.
ROAD
ROSETTI RD.
CASTLERS RD.
NORMAN RD.
VAL PRINSEPS RD.
Martello Tower no.60
PEVENSEY BAY
A259
INNINGS DRIVE
THE BEACHINGS
EASTBOURNE RD.
GRENVILLE RD.
CADOGAN CT.
TIMBERLAINE RD.
MILLWARD RD.
CLARENCE CT.
RAGLAN CT.
Martello Tower no.61
EASTBOURNE
MARTELLO BEACH CARAVAN PARK
GREY TOWER RD
GREY TOWER CARAVAN SITE
Martello Tower no.62
GREY TOWERS BUNGALOWS
Bay View Golf Course
Pevensey Bay Sailing Club
BAY VIEW
A B C D
1 2 3 4 5 6
11
17
565 66
06 05 04 03

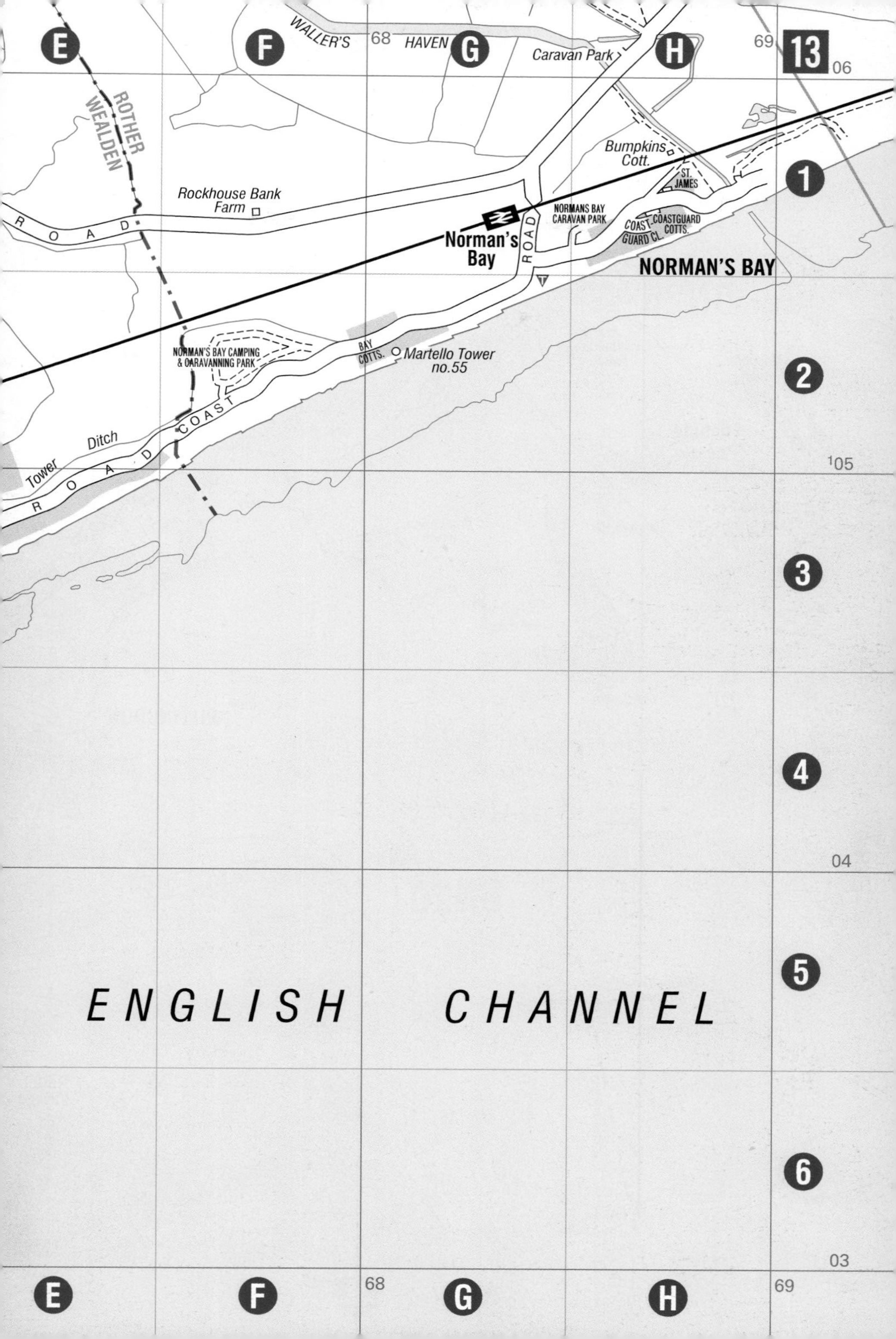

E
F
WALLER'S
68
HAVEN
G
Caravan Park
H
69
06
ROTHER
WEALDEN
Bumpkins Cott.
ST. JAMES
1
Rockhouse Bank Farm
ROAD
NORMANS BAY CARAVAN PARK
COAST GUARD CL.
COASTGUARD COTTS.
Norman's Bay
ROAD
NORMAN'S BAY
NORMAN'S BAY CAMPING & CARAVANNING PARK
BAY COTTS.
Martello Tower no.55
2
COAST
Ditch
Tower
ROAD
105
3
4
04
ENGLISH CHANNEL
5
6
03
E
F
68
G
H
69

14
8
18
A
B
C
D
1
2
3
4
5
6
57
58
04
03
102
01
Polegate
WANNOCK
WILLINGDON
BN26
BN20
SOUTH DOWNS NATIONAL PARK
Wannock Coppice
Willingdon Community School
Willingdon Prim. Sch.
Tower-mill
Fields
Pav.
Willows Farm
Foulride Green
Rec. Grd.
Lib.
Crane Down
Wannock Glen
Wannock Place
Wannock Farm
Filching
Campbell Circuit
Filching Manor
Dean Wood
Hanging Hill
Willingdon Links
Cemetery
The Combe
Tas Combe
Helling Down
Butt's Brow
Combe Hill
Cold Crouch
Chalk Farm
The Plantation
Babylon Down
Beehive Plantation
Marcia Dene
Butts Brow Memorial
Willingdon Bottom
Ratton Village
WILLINGDON
GOLF COURSE
Club Hous
Bourne Hill
Harewick Bottom
WEALDEN
EASTBOURNE
EASTBOURNE ROAD
A2270
JEVINGTON
WAYFARING DOWN
BABYLON
TRACK
WANNOCK LANE
WANNOCK ROAD
WANNOCK RD.
WANNOCK AV.
WANNOCK GDNS.
CORNMILL GDNS.
MILL WY.
OLD MILL LANE
MILL CL.
BROADWATER MS.
GLEN CL.
GLEN COTTS.
HONEYWAY
FILCHING CL.
LANCING WY.
MORTIMER GDNS.
MILLSTREAM GDNS.
PADDOCK GDS.
MAYFAIR CL.
FARMLANDS AV.
FARMLANDS WY.
FARMLANDS CL.
FARMLANDS CT.
THE MILLRACE
SOUTHFIELD
GROSVENOR CL.
TOWER MILL PL.
WINDMILL PL.
CROFT
PARK CROFT
CL.
COPPICE AV.
COPPICE CL.
CHURCH CL.
BROADVIEW CL.
DOWNSVALLEY RD.
OLDFIELD ROAD
OLDFIELD AV.
TOTT YEW RD.
THURROCK CL.
WILLINGDON CT.
SCANLAN CL.
ORCHARD PDE.
THE TRIANGLE
DOWNSVIEW RD.
SOUTHDOWN AV.
SOUTHDOWN COTTS.
RAPSON'S RD.
THE CRESCENT
QUEENS RIDE
THE GROVE
THE PARAGON
BROCKS GHYLL
HAZEL GRO.
AVENUE
GORRINGE VALLEY RD.
GORRINGE DR.
GORRINGE CL.
THE DENE
CARMEN CT.
MEWETT'S CT.
MEACHANTS LA.
MEACHANTS CT.
COMBE RISE
PORTSDOWN WY.
MANOR CL.
COOPERS WY.
COOPERS CROFT
GOODWOOD CL.
TAS COMBE WY.
THE CROFT
CHURCH
HILL
WALK FARM CL.
THE LAWNS
OLD BARN CL.
HOCKINGTON LANE
CROUCH CL.
WISH HILL
UPPER
ANGUS CL.
WEDDERBURN RD.
BUCKHURST CL.
BADGE
MELVILL
PARKWAY
BUTTS
OLD MANSION CL.
UPPER RATTON DR.
UPPER RATTON
MARCIA CL.
BABYLON
THE CLOSE
MANOR WY.
THE COMBE
THE GROVE
LINKWAY
RATTON DR.
OXENDEAN GDNS.
WINDOVER WY.
BAILEY CRES.
ST. ANNES ROAD
SEVEN SISTERS RD.
SHORT BROW CL.
HAMLA
WENT HILL GS.
THE MARTLETS
Rec. Grd.
MEADOW
HUGGETTS
ST. MARY'S CL.
CLEEVELANDS
THE LAWNS
WESTMORLAND
SHROPSHIRE
LINCOLN C
ESSEX CT.
HAM CT.

15
16
9
19
LOWER WILLINGDON
HAMPDEN PARK
Eastbourne
BN22
BN21
GOLDEN JUBILEE WAY
A22
CROSS LEVELS WAY
A2280
KING'S DRIVE
A2021
A2270
Hampden Park
The Eastbourne Academy
The Lindfield School
Hampden Pk. Sports Cen.
Parkland Jun. & Inf. Schs.
Oakwood Sch.
Comm. Cen.
Hampden Park Inf. Sch.
Decoy Wood
Decoy Pond
Eastbourne Indoor Bowls Club
David Lloyd Leisure
Trax Indoor Karting Cen.
Superstore
St. Wilfrids Hospice (open late 2013)
Eastbourne Sports Park
Running Track
Sussex Downs College
EASTBOURNE DISTRICT GENERAL HOSPITAL
Ratton School
Eastbourne Tutorial Unit
The Coppice
Shinewater Lake
Southbourne Lake
EASTBOURNE GOLFING PARK
Elm Grove Smallholdings
Rugby Pitch
Rugby Club
Playing Fields
Playing Field
Rec. Grd.
Willingdon & West Langney Sewer
BRODRICK ROAD
PARKFIELD AVENUE
BRASSEY AVENUE
DECOY DRIVE
ROSEBERY AVENUE
LOTTBRIDGE DROVE
WILLINGDON ROAD
ROTTINGDEAN ROAD

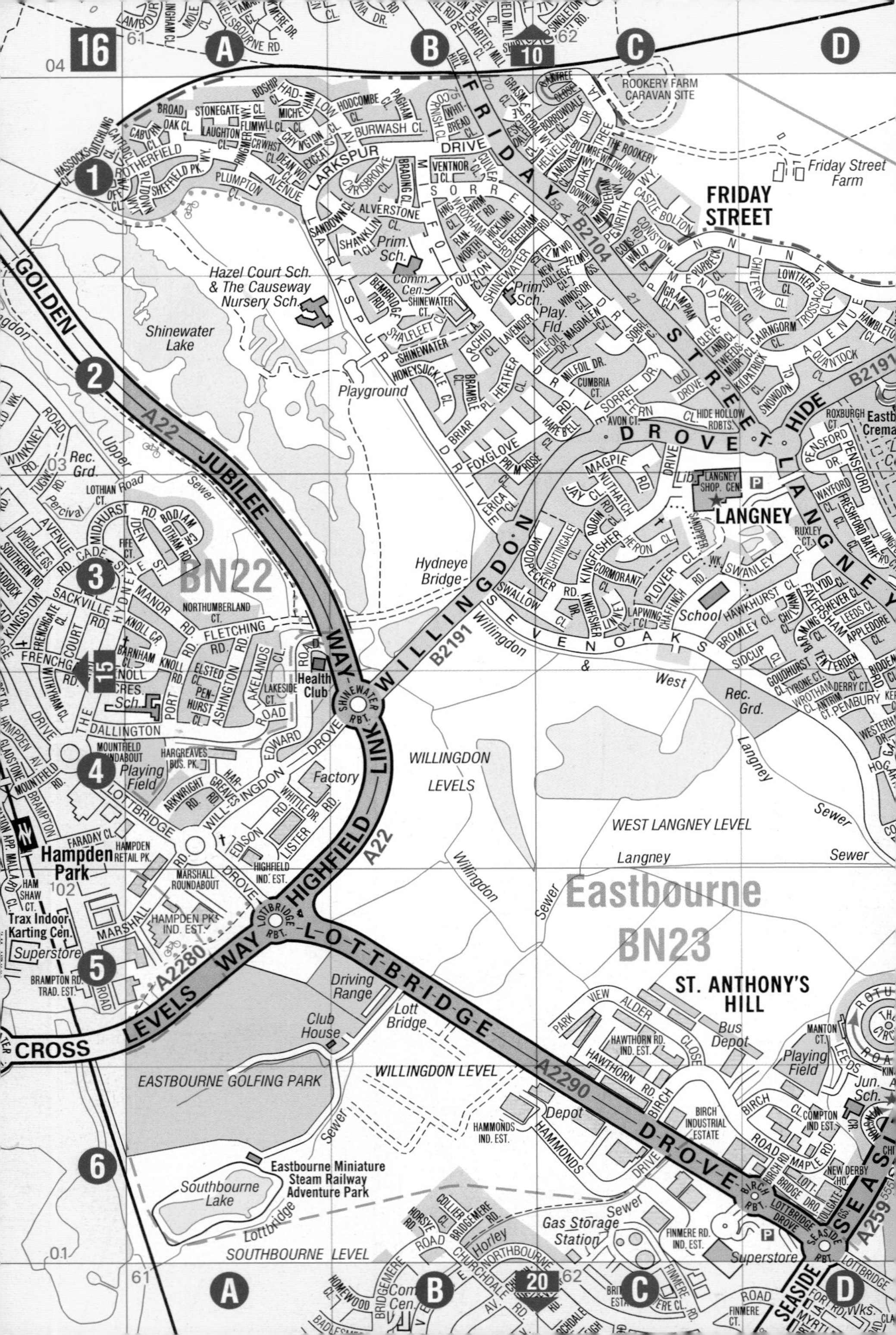

16
A
B
C
D
10
04
61
62
1
2
3
4
5
6
ROOKERY FARM CARAVAN SITE
Friday Street Farm
FRIDAY STREET
FRIDAY
STREET
B2104
LARKSPUR
AVENUE
DRIVE
ROTHERFIELD
SHEFFIELD PK.
PLUMPTON
HASSOCKS CL.
DITCHLING
BURWASH CL.
HODCOMBE CL.
PAGHAM
VENTNOR CL.
CARISBROOKE
BRADING CL.
ALVERSTONE
SANDOWN CL.
SHANKLIN CL.
Prim. Sch.
Comm. Cen.
SHINEWATER CT.
SHINEWATER LA.
SHALFLEET CL.
BEMBRIDGE
HONEYSUCKLE CL.
BRAMBLE CL.
HEATHER
BRIAR PL.
FOXGLOVE
PRIMROSE
ERICA CL.
HAREBELL
MILFOIL DR.
MAGDALEN
WINDSOR CL.
NEW COLLEGE CL.
Play. Fld.
CUMBRIA CT.
SORREL DR.
OLD DROVE
HIDE HOLLOW RDBTS.
AVON CT.
THE ROOKERY
WILDWOOD
PENRITH WY.
CASTLE BOLTON
CONISTON
PENNINE
MENDIP
PURBECK
GRAMPIAN
CHEVIOT CL.
CHILTERN
LOWTHER CL.
TROSSACHS
CAIRNGORM CL.
QUANTOCK
SNOWDON
KILPATRICK
CLEVELAND CL.
TWEEDSMUIR
HAMBLETON
AVENUE
HIDE
B2191
DROVE
LANGNEY
ROXBURGH CT.
PENSFORD
WAYFORD
FRESHFORD
BATHFORD
RUXLEY CT.
LANGNEY SHOP. CEN.
Lib.
LANGNEY
MAGPIE
NUTHATCH
JAY CL.
ROBIN
HERON CL.
KINGFISHER
CORMORANT
SANDPIPER
PLOVER
SWANLEY
LAPWING CL.
CHAFFINCH
WOODPECKER
NIGHTINGALE
SWALLOW
School
HAWKHURST CL.
BROMLEY CL.
CHIDDINGSTONE
SIDCUP CL.
SEVENOAKS
FAVERSHAM
LYDD CL.
HEVER CL.
LEEDS CL.
APPLEDORE
TENTERDEN
GOUDHURST
TYRONE CT.
WROTHAM CL.
DERRY CT.
ANTRIM CT.
PEMBURY
BIDDENDEN
WESTERHAM
Rec. Grd.
Willingdon & West Langney Sewer
WILLINGDON
B2191
Hydneye Bridge
Hazel Court Sch. & The Causeway Nursery Sch.
Shinewater Lake
Playground
BN22
GOLDEN
A22
JUBILEE WAY
SHINEWATER RBT.
Health Club
LAKESIDE CT.
AKELANDS
ASHINGTON
FLETCHING
NORTHUMBERLAND CT.
MANOR
HYDNEYE
MIDHURST RD.
BODIAM
OTHAM
FIFE CT.
CADE
SACKVILLE RD.
KNOLL CR.
KNOLL CRES.
BARNHAM
ELSTED CL.
PENHURST CL.
PORT RD.
Sch.
15
FRENCHGATE
COURT
WITHYHAM CL.
KINGSTON
SOUTHERN RD.
DOVEDALE GS.
AVENUE
LOTHIAN Road CT.
Percival
Upper
Sewer
Rec. Grd.
WINKNEY RD.
ROAD
03
DALLINGTON
THE DRIVE
MOUNTFIELD ROUNDABOUT
MOUNTFIELD RD.
Playing Field
HARGREAVES BUS. PK.
ARKWRIGHT RD.
WILLINGDON DROVE
EDWARD
Factory
WHITTLE DR.
LISTER RD.
EDISON RD.
LOTTBRIDGE
MARSHALL ROUNDABOUT
HIGHFIELD IND. EST.
HIGHFIELD LINK
HAMPDEN RETAIL PK.
FARADAY CL.
Hampden Park
102
BRAMPTON
HAMPDEN AV.
GLADSTONE
HAMSHAW CT.
Trax Indoor Karting Cen.
Superstore
MARSHALL
HAMPDEN PK. IND. EST.
BRAMPTON RD. TRAD. EST.
A2280
LEVELS WAY
CROSS
LOTTBRIDGE RBT.
LOTTBRIDGE DROVE
WILLINGDON LEVELS
WEST LANGNEY LEVEL
Langney Sewer
Eastbourne
BN23
ST. ANTHONY'S HILL
PARK VIEW
ALDER CLOSE
HAWTHORN RD. IND. EST.
HAWTHORN RD.
BIRCH
Bus Depot
Playing Field
MANTON CT.
Jun. Sch.
COMPTON IND. EST.
BIRCH INDUSTRIAL ESTATE
MAPLE RD.
NEW DERBY HO.
BIRCH RBT.
SEASIDE RBT.
SEASIDE
A259
A2290
DROVE
Depot
HAMMONDS IND. EST.
HAMMONDS DRIVE
Driving Range
Club House
Lott Bridge
EASTBOURNE GOLFING PARK
WILLINGDON LEVEL
Eastbourne Miniature Steam Railway Adventure Park
Southbourne Lake
Lottbridge
SOUTHBOURNE LEVEL
Gas Storage Station
Sewer
FINMERE RD. IND. EST.
Superstore
COLLIER CL.
BRIDGEMERE RD.
HORSYE RD.
ROAD
Horley
NORTHBOURNE
CHURCHDALE
BRIDGEMERE
HOMEWOOD CL.
Comm. Cen.
20
01
61
62
FINMERE CT.
ROAD

E
F
G
H
17
11
12
21
1
2
3
4
5
6
Pevensey
BN24
MOUNTNEY LEVEL
Mountney Bridge
POTTS MARSH INDUSTRIAL ESTATE
WESTHAM BUSINESS PARK
MOUNTNEY BRIDGE BUSINESS PARK
FAIRFIELDS FARM CARAVAN
Fairfield Farm
Mountney Sewer
Mill Ditch
HIDE HOLLOW
EASTBOURNE RD.
B2191
PRIORY RBT.
East Langney Sewer
PRIORY LANE
WEALDEN
EASTBOURNE
Langney Sports Club
Eastbourne Borough FC (Priory Lane Stadium)
EAST LANGNEY LEVEL
LANGNEY SEWER
CASTLE VIEW CARAVAN AND CAMPING SITE
MARTELLO BEACH CARAVAN PARK
GREY TOWER ROAD
GREY TOWER CARAVAN SITE
Martello Tower no.62
GREY TOWER BUNGALOWS
Bay View Golf Course
Pevensey Bay Sailing Club
BAY VIEW CAMPING AND CARAVANNING PARK
OLD MARTELLO ROAD
The German's
EASTBOURNE ROAD
A259
PEVENSEY BAY ROAD
MARTELLO RDBT.
HARBOUR RDBT.
LANGNEY RBT.
GOLDING ROAD
NETHERFIELD
TOLKIEN ROAD
FLEMING CL.
DURRELL CL.
Playing Fields
Langney Village
Sch.
MONARCH GDNS.
Fitness First
Cineworld Cinema
SOVEREIGN HARBOUR RETAIL PARK
The Crumbles
PACIFIC DRIVE
HARBOUR QUAY
Sovereign Harbour Yacht Club
HARBOUR CLUB APTS.
PACIFIC HEIGHTS NORTH
PACIFIC HEIGHTS SOUTH
Martello Tower no.64
SOVEREIGN HARBOUR
TRUJILLO CT.
HAMILTON QUAY
THE WATERFRONT
RAPALA CT.
PALOMAR CT.
FIADOR CT.
CENTAURI CT.
BIMINI CT.
ORVIS CT.
MIDWAY QUAY
Sovereign Harbour Marina
Lifeboat Station
Outer Harbour
Breakwater
Sovereign Harbour
Breakwater
ENGLISH CHANNEL
ATLANTIC DRIVE
SAN JUAN COURT
DOMINICA CT.
ANGUILLA CL.
MONSERRAT VS.
BERMUDA MEWS
Martello Tower no. 66
LANGNEY POINT RDBTS.
Works
Langney Point Outfall
PRINCES ROAD
MOUNTBATTEN DR.
04
03
02
01
565
64

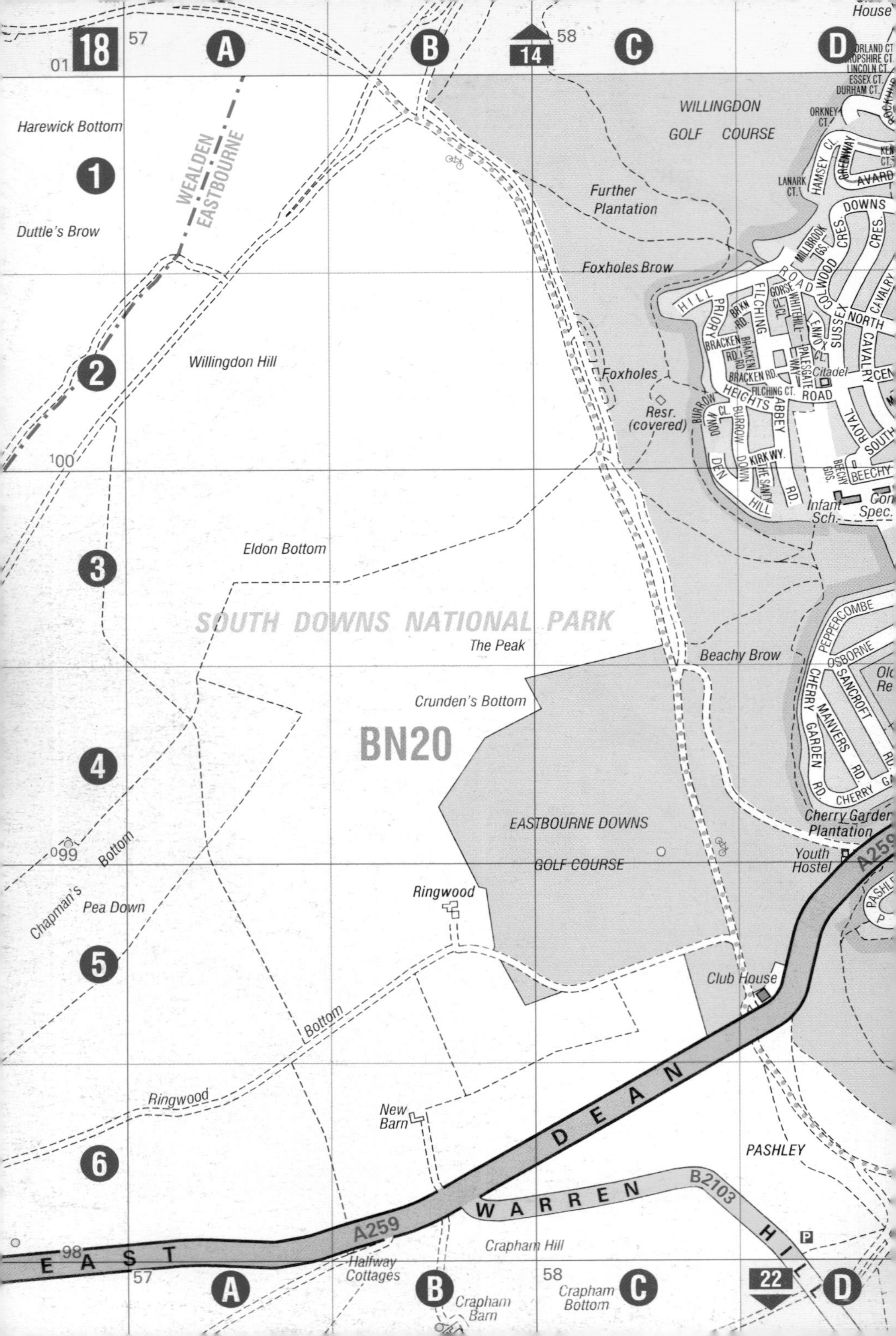
18
14
22
A
B
C
D
1
2
3
4
5
6
57
58
01
100
99
98
Harewick Bottom
Duttle's Brow
WEALDEN
EASTBOURNE
Willingdon Hill
WILLINGDON
GOLF COURSE
Further Plantation
Foxholes Brow
Foxholes
Resr. (covered)
Eldon Bottom
SOUTH DOWNS NATIONAL PARK
The Peak
Beachy Brow
Crunden's Bottom
BN20
EASTBOURNE DOWNS
GOLF COURSE
Chapman's Bottom
Pea Down
Ringwood
Bottom
Ringwood
New Barn
Club House
Youth Hostel
Cherry Garden Plantation
PASHLEY
EAST DEAN
A259
WARREN HILL
B2103
Crapham Hill
Halfway Cottages
Crapham Barn
Crapham Bottom
Infant Sch.
Citadel
FILCHING RD.
PRIORY HEIGHTS
BURROW DOWN
ABBEY RD.
KIRK WY.
SUSSEX
NORTH CAVALRY
ROYAL SOUTH
BEECHY AVE.
PEPPERCOMBE
OSBORNE
SANCROFT
MANVERS RD.
CHERRY GARDEN RD.
DOWNS CRES.
COLWOOD CRES.
MILLBROOK GDS.
HAMSEY CL.
GREENWAY
AVARD
LANARK CT.
ORKNEY CT.
ESSEX CT.
DURHAM CT.
LINCOLN CT.
SHROPSHIRE CT.
MORLAND CT.
House

15
19
20
23
2
E
F
G
H
1
2
3
4
5
6
BN22
BN21
EASTBOURNE DISTRICT GENERAL HOSPITAL
Hosp. Accom.
Playing Field
KING'S DRIVE
LEVELS WAY
A2280
A2021
A2270
A259
RODMILL RBT.
CROSS LEVELS
WILLINGDON ROAD
EASTBOURNE LEVEL
Lottbridge
Upperton Farm
Poultry Farm
St. Thomas a Becket Cath. Jun. & Inf. Schs.
The Cavendish School
Cavendish Sports Centre
Motcombe Inf. Sch.
Cemetery
UPPERTON
UPPERTON ROAD
LEWES RD.
PRIDEAUX ROAD
ROBOROUGH DAY HOSP.
THE AVENUE
Hartfield Sq.
CHURCH ST.
HIGH ST.
THE GOFFS
OLD TOWN
Mnr. Gds.
Bowl. Grns.
Gildredge Park
Temple Grove
Sports Grd.
War. Meml. Fld.
Eastbourne
Club House
ROYAL EASTBOURNE GOLF COURSE
EASTBOURNE
Compton Place
Compton Park
The Saffrons
Town Hall
Eastbourne College
Devonshire Park
Towner
Thtres.
EASTBOURNE
TERMINUS RD.
GILDREDGE RD.
SOUTH ST.
Paradise Plantation
Reservoir (covered)
Moira House Schools
Univ of Brighton (Welkin Site)
Univ. of Brighton (Hillbrow)
Trevin Towers
Tennis Courts
MEADS
Warren
PARADISE DRIVE
CARLISLE RD.
KING EDWARDS PARADE
Depot
Lake
SOUTHBOU

20
16
19
3
A
B
C
D
1
2
3
4
5
6
SOUTHBOURNE LEVEL
EASTBOURNE LEVEL
Lottbridge
ROSELANDS
BN22
BN21
Eastbourne
EASTBOURNE
Stafford Jun. Sch.
Upperton Farm
Poultry Farm
St. Thomas a Becket Cath. Jun. & Inf. Sch.
Southbourne Bus. Park
Roselands Infant Sch.
Superstore
Finmere Rd. Ind. Est.
Britland Estate
The Oval
Crumbles Pond
Princes
The Lawns
Lifeboat Station
Lifeboat Launching
Treasure Island Adventure Park
Redoubt Fortress & Military Museum
Glennys Ind. Est.
Arndale Cen.
Eastbourne Pier
Eastbourne Bandstand
Eastbourne Lifeboat Museum
The Wish Tower (Martello Tower no.73)
Western Lawns
Devonshire Park
Eastbourne College
Towner
Ten. Cen.
A2021
A259
B2103
WHITLEY ROAD
SEASIDE
ROYAL PDE.
MARINE PARADE
GRAND PDE.
KING EDWARDS PDE.
LEWES RD.
UPPER AVENUE
THE AVENUE
ASHFORD RD.
SUSAN'S RD.
TRINITY TREES
TERMINUS RD.
DEVONSHIRE PL.
SOUTH ST.
GILDREDGE RD.
CARLISLE ROAD
COMPTON ST.
BEACH RD.
SEAFORD ROAD
CHANNEL VIEW RD.
NORTHBOURNE ROAD
SOUTHBOURNE RD.
ROSELANDS AVENUE
ST. PHILIPS AVENUE
RINGWOOD ROAD
BRIDGEMERE RD.
CHURCHDALE RD.
LOTTBRIDGE DROVE
LANGNEY ROAD
CAVENDISH PL.
PROMENADE
EAST-BOURNE
62
61
100
99
98

21
E
F
G
H
17
64
565
01
BN23
PRINCES
ROAD
JERVIS
COLLINGWOOD CL.
PRINCE
WILLIAM
BLAKES
WAY
FROBISHER CL.
HOOD CL.
RALEIGH CL.
MOUNTBATTEN DR.
RAMSAY
SCHOFIELD
PARADE
Works
PROMENADE
Langney Point
Outfall
Sovereign
Park
Sovereign
Centre
MONARCH HO.
Fun
1
2
100
3
ENGLISH
CHANNEL
4
099
5
6
98
E
F
64
G
H
565

22
INSET
A
B
C
D
18
Field House Farm
Friston Down
FRISTON
Eastbourne
BN20
Summer Down
Warren Hill
WARREN HILL
B2103
FRISTON PLACE
Friston Down
Black Robin Farm
SEAFORD RD.
FRISTON HILL
A259
EASTBOURNE ROAD
EAST DEAN RD.
Eastdean Down
Paynes Dene
Point House
Hobb's Eares
War Mem.
Hall
EAST DEAN
CHURCHFIELD
SOUTH DOWNS NATIONAL PARK
Bullock Down Farm House
The Cott
Pav.
Rec. Grd.
Went Hill
WEALDEN
EASTBOURNE
Seven Sisters Sheep Centre
Birling Lodge
Heathy
Frost Hill
West Brow
Coas
Beachy Head Countryside C
Hodcombe Farm
Hod Combe
BEACHY HEAD
Shooters' Bottom
Beachy Head Lighthouse
1
2
3
4
5
6
55
56
57
58
99
98
96
95

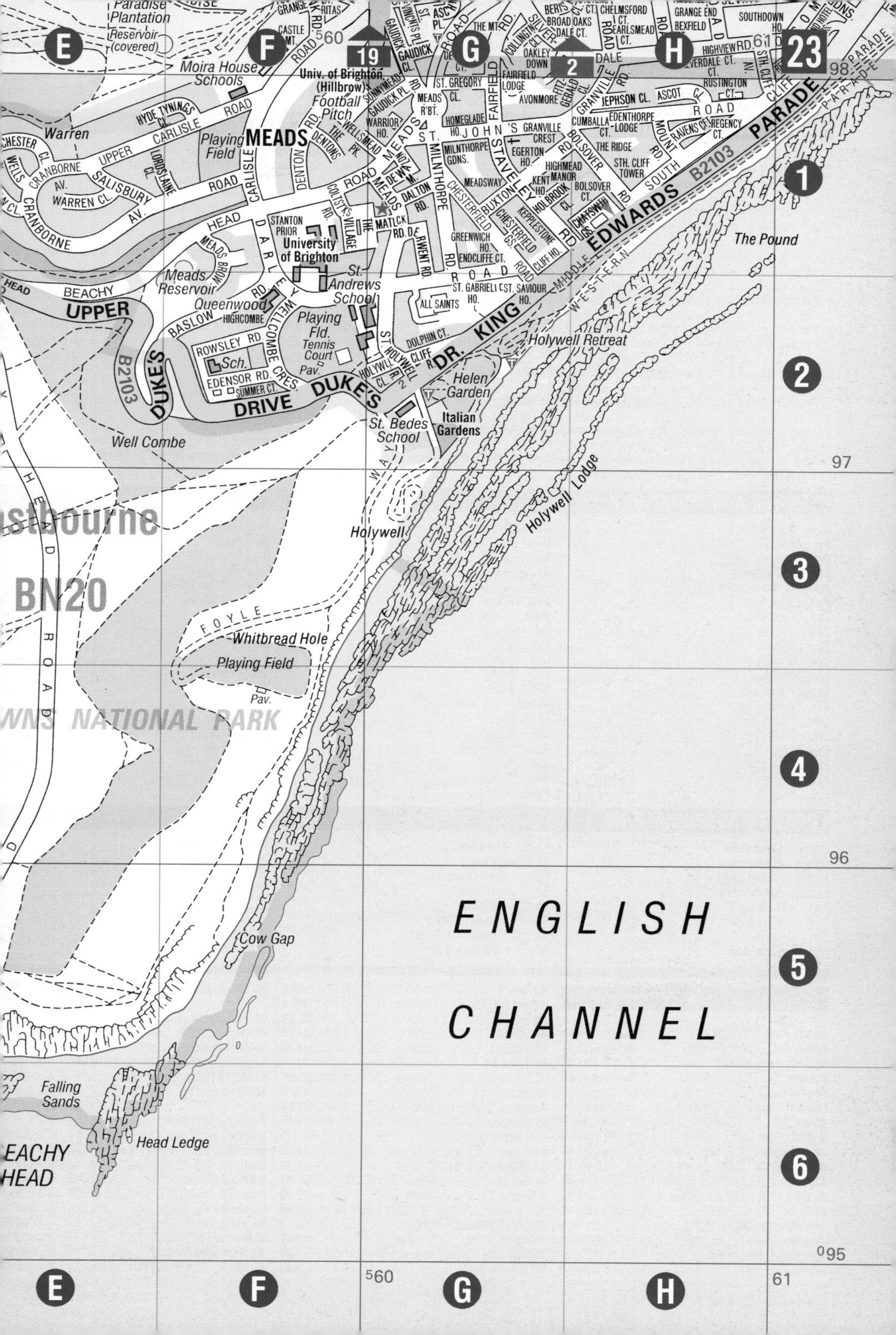

E
F
G
H
19
2
23
1
2
3
4
5
6
560
61
98
97
96
95
Paradise Plantation
Reservoir (covered)
Moira House Schools
Univ. of Brighton (Hillbrow)
Football Pitch
Warren
Playing Field
MEADS
HYDE TYNINGS CL.
CARLISLE ROAD
UPPER CARLISLE
CHESTER CL.
WELLS
CRANBORNE AV.
SALISBURY ROAD
LORDSLAINE CL.
WARREN CL.
CRANBORNE AV.
MEADS BROW
Meads Reservoir
UNIVERSITY of Brighton
STANTON PRIOR
St. Andrews School
COLSTOCKS VILLAGE
DENTON RD.
THE PK.
WELLSMEAD
WARRIOR HO.
MEADS RD.
DEWAR M.
MATLOCK RD.
DALTON RD.
DERWENT RD.
ST. JOHN'S ROAD
MILNTHORPE RD.
MILNTHORPE GDNS.
MEADSWAY
HOMEGLADE HO.
ST. GREGORY CL.
MEADS R'BT.
GAUDICK PL.
GAUDICK CL.
SUNNYMEAD
CHESTERFIELD RD.
CHESTERFIELD GS.
GREENWICH HO.
ENDCLIFFE CT.
BUXTON RD.
STAVELEY RD.
KEPPLESTONE
CLIFF HO.
KENT HO.
HOLBROOK CL.
HIGHMEAD MANOR
EGERTON HO.
GRANVILLE CREST
BOLSOVER RD.
BOLSOVER CT.
CHATSWORTH GS.
AVONMORE
FAIRFIELD LODGE
FAIRFIELD
FITZGERALD CL.
GRANVILLE RD.
CUMBALLA CT.
EDENTHORPE LODGE
THE RIDGE
STH. CLIFF TOWER
JEPHSON CL.
ASCOT CL.
MOUNT RD.
RAVENS CFT.
REGENCY CT.
RUSTINGTON CT.
SILVERDALE CT.
HIGHVIEW RD.
SOUTHDOWN HO.
GRANGE END
BEXFIELD
CHELMSFORD CT.
EARLSMEAD CT.
BROAD OAKS
DALE CT.
OAKLEY DOWN
COLLINGTON
THE MT.
DALE
SOUTH CLIFF
PARADE
ST. GABRIEL CT.
ST. SAVIOUR HO.
ALL SAINTS
DOLPHIN CT.
ST. HOLYWELL CLIFF RD.
HOLYWELL CL.
DR. KING EDWARDS PARADE
B2103
MIDDLE WESTERN
The Pound
Holywell Retreat
Helen Garden
Italian Gardens
St. Bedes School
WAY
Holywell
Holywell Lodge
BEACHY HEAD
UPPER DUKE'S DRIVE
DUKE'S
Queenwood
HIGHCOMBE
BASLOW RD.
DARLEY RD.
WELLCOMBE CRES.
ROWSLEY RD.
Sch.
EDENSOR RD.
SUMMER CT.
Playing Fld.
Tennis Court
Pav.
Well Combe
Eastbourne
BN20
BEACHY HEAD ROAD
FOYLE
Whitbread Hole
Playing Field
Pav.
DOWNS NATIONAL PARK
ENGLISH CHANNEL
Cow Gap
Falling Sands
Head Ledge
BEACHY HEAD

INDEX

Including Streets, Places & Areas, Hospitals etc., Industrial Estates, Selected Flats & Walkways, Stations and Selected Places of Interest.

HOW TO USE THIS INDEX

1. Each street name is followed by its Postcode District, then by its Locality abbreviation(s) and then by its map reference; e.g. **Albert Rd.** BN26: Pole . . . .4B **8** is in the BN26 Postcode District and the Polegate Locality and is to be found in square 4B on page **8**. The page number is shown in bold type.

2. A strict alphabetical order is followed in which Av., Rd., St., etc. (though abbreviated) are read in full and as part of the street name; e.g. **Ash Gro.** appears after **Ashgate Rd.** but before **Ashington Rd.**

3. Streets and a selection of flats and walkways that cannot be shown on the mapping, appear in the index with the thoroughfare to which they are connected shown in brackets; e.g. **Archery Ct.** *BN22: Eastb . . . .1C **20** (off Willoughby Cres.)*

4. Addresses that are in more than one part are referred to as not continuous.

5. Places and areas are shown in the index in **BLUE TYPE** and the map reference is to the actual map square in which the town centre or area is located and not to the place name shown on the map; e.g. **HANKHAM 3B 10**

6. An example of a selected place of interest is **Anderida Roman Fort 5G 11**

7. An example of a station is **Hampden Park Station (Rail) 4H 15**

8. An example of a Hospital, Hospice or selected Healthcare facility is **AMBERSTONE HOSPITAL 3G 5**

9. Map references for entries that appear on large scale pages **2-3** are shown first, with small scale map references shown in brackets; e.g. **Alciston M.** BN21: Eastb 3F **3** (5A **20**)

GENERAL ABBREVIATIONS

App. : Approach
Av. : Avenue
Bri. : Bridge
Bldgs. : Buildings
Bungs. : Bungalows
Bus. : Business
Cvn. : Caravan
Cen. : Centre
Cl. : Close
Coll. : College
Cott. : Cottage
Cotts. : Cottages
Ct. : Court
Cres. : Crescent
Cft. : Croft
Dr. : Drive
E. : East
Est. : Estate
Fld. : Field
Gdn. : Garden
Gdns. : Gardens
Ga. : Gate
Gt. : Great
Grn. : Green
Gro. : Grove
Hgts. : Heights
Ho. : House
Ind. : Industrial
Info. : Information
La. : Lane
Mnr. : Manor
Mans. : Mansions
M. : Mews
Mt. : Mount
Mus. : Museum
Nth. : North
No. : Number
Pde. : Parade
Pk. : Park
Pl. : Place
Ri. : Rise
Rd. : Road
Rdbt. : Roundabout
Shop. : Shopping
Sth. : South
Sq. : Square
St. : Street
Ter. : Terrace
Twr. : Tower
Trad. : Trading
Up. : Upper
Vw. : View
Vs. : Villas
Wlk. : Walk
W. : West
Yd. : Yard

LOCALITY ABBREVIATIONS

Cowb : **Cowbeech**
Down : **Downash**
E Dean : **East Dean**
Eastb : **Eastbourne**
Filch : **Filching**
Folk : **Folkington**
Fris : **Friston**
Hails : **Hailsham**
Hank : **Hankham**
Hell : **Hellingly**
Herst : **Herstmonceux**
Jev : **Jevington**
Lang : **Langney**
Lwr D : **Lower Dicker**
Mag D : **Magham Down**
Nor B : **Norman's Bay**
Pev : **Pevensey**
Pev B : **Pevensey Bay**
Pole : **Polegate**
Rick : **Rickney**
Sto C : **Stone Cross**
Wart : **Wartling**
W'ham : **Westham**
Will : **Willingdon**

A

Abbey Path BN27: Hails 5E **5**
Abbey Rd. BN20: Eastb 2D **18**
Abbot's Lodge BN21: Eastb 3H **19**
Abbotts Cl. BN22: Eastb 3A **20**
Aberdale Rd. BN26: Pole 5E **9**
Acacia Rd. BN22: Eastb 3F **15**
Acorn Grn. BN27: Hails 6D **4**
Acorns, The BN27: Hails 2F **7**
Addingham Rd. BN22: Eastb 3C **20**
Admiralty Ct. BN23: Eastb 4H **17**
Admiralty Cres. BN23: Eastb 3H **17**
Admiralty Way BN23: Eastb 4H **17**
Adur Dr. BN24: Sto C 6A **10**
Akehurst Cl. BN27: Hell 1F **5**
Alastair Ct. BN21: Eastb 6E **3**
Albany Ct. BN21: Eastb 2H **19**
Albert Pde. BN21: Eastb 2E **19**
Albert Pl. BN26: Pole 4C **8**
Albert Rd. BN26: Pole 4B **8**
Albert Ter. BN21: Eastb 2E **19**
Albion Rd. BN22: Eastb 3B **20**
Alcazar Ct. BN21: Eastb 3H **19**
Alciston M.
BN21: Eastb 3F **3** (5A **20**)
Aldenham Ct. BN21: Eastb 2D **2**
Alder Cl. BN23: Eastb 5C **16**
Alexandra Ct.
BN21: Eastb 1C **2** (4H **19**)
Alexandra Ho. BN21: Eastb 1C **2**
Alexandra Rd. BN22: Eastb 1D **20**
Alfred Rd. BN23: Eastb 5F **17**
Alfriston Cl. BN20: Eastb 5E **19**
Alice Hudson Gdns. BN23: Eastb 6D **16**
Allchorn Pleasure Boats 3G **3**
Allesley BN20: Eastb 6A **2**
Allfrey Rd. BN22: Eastb 1D **20**
All Saints BN20: Eastb 2G **23**
All Souls Brass Rubbing Cen. . . . . *.2F 3*
(off Susan's Rd.
Alverstone Cl. BN23: Lang 1B **16**
Amberley BN21: Eastb 6D **2** (6H **19**)
Amberley Rd. BN22: Will 4E **15**
AMBERSTONE 4G **5**
AMBERSTONE HOSPITAL 3G **5**
Amberstone Vw. BN27: Hails 4E **5**
(not continuous)
Ancaster Ho. BN21: Eastb 6E **3**
Anchorage Way BN23: Eastb 3H **17**
Anderida BN21: Eastb 1D **2** (3H **19**)
Anderida Rd. BN22: Eastb, Will 2D **14**
Anderida Roman Fort 5G **1**
Andwell Ct. BN21: Eastb 3G **3**
Anglesey Av. BN27: Hails 5C **4**
Anguilla Cl. BN23: Eastb 6G **17**
Angus Cl. BN20: Will 4D **14**
Annington Rd. BN22: Eastb 2B **2**
Anson Cl. BN23: Eastb 6E **1**

Antares Path BN27: Hails .2G **7**
Antigua Cl. BN23: Eastb .5F **17**
Antrim Ct. BN23: Lang .4D **16**
Apex Pk. BN27: Hails .2C **6**
(not continuous)
Apex Way BN27: Hails .2C **6**
Appledore Cl. BN23: Lang .3D **16**
Archery Ct. *BN22: Eastb .1C 20*
(off Willoughby Cres.)
Archery La. BN22: Eastb .1D **20**
Archery Wlk. BN27: Hails .2E **7**
Ardarragh Mans. BN22: Eastb .3A **20**
Arequipa Reef BN23: Eastb .5G **17**
Argyle Ct. BN22: Eastb .3G **15**
Arkwright Rd. BN23: Eastb .4A **16**
Arlington Eagles Rdbt.
BN27: Hails .4B **6**
Arlington Ho. *BN21: Eastb .3G 19*
(off Upperton Rd.)
Arlington Lodge BN21: Eastb .3F **3**
Arlington Rd. BN21: Eastb .2C **2** (4H **19**)
Arlington Rd. E. BN27: Hails .3C **6**
Arlington Rd. W. BN27: Hails .3A **6**
Arlington Stadium (Speedway) .3A **6**
Arnworth Ct. BN21: Eastb .4D **2** (5H **19**)
Arran Cl. BN27: Hails .5C **4**
Arrow Dr. BN27: Hails .5E **5**
Artisans Dwellings
BN21: Eastb .3D **2**
Arun Cl. *BN24: Sto C .6H 9*
(off Arun Way)
Arundel Cl. BN24: Pev B .3D **12**
BN27: Hails .5E **5**
Arundel Ct. BN21: Eastb .3H **19**
Arundel Ho. BN21: Eastb .1C **2**
(Hartfield Rd.)
BN21: Eastb .1B **2**
(Michel Gro.)
Arundel Keep BN21: Eastb .3H **19**
Arundel Rd. BN21: Eastb .1B **2** (3H **19**)
Arun Lodge BN21: Eastb .1B **2**
Arun Way BN24: Sto C .6H **9**
Ascham Pl. BN20: Eastb .6A **2** (6G **19**)
Ascot Cl. BN20: Eastb .6C **2** (1H **23**)
Ashampstead Pl. BN21: Eastb .1C **2**
Ashbourne Ct. BN21: Eastb .4F **3**
Ashburnham Gdns.
BN21: Eastb .2G **19**
Ashburnham Pl. BN27: Hails .5C **4**
Ashburnham Rd. BN21: Eastb .3G **19**
Ash Cl. BN22: Eastb .2G **15**
Ash Ct. BN27: Hails .2C **6**
Ashford Cl. BN27: Hails .2E **7**
Ashford Rd. BN21: Eastb .2E **3** (4A **20**)
Ashford Sq. BN21: Eastb .1F **3** (4A **20**)
Ashgate Rd. BN23: Lang .3E **17**
Ash Gro. BN24: W'ham .5D **10**
Ashington Rd. BN22: Eastb .4A **16**
Ashley Gdns. *BN22: Eastb .1C 20*
(off Willoughby Cres.)
BN27: Hails .4E **5**
Aspen Rd. BN22: Eastb .3G **15**
Astaire Av. BN22: Eastb .2B **20**
Astaire Cl. BN22: Eastb .1B **20**
Athelstan Cl. BN23: Eastb .4F **17**
Atlantic Dr. BN23: Eastb .5F **17**
Attfield Wlk. BN22: Eastb .2H **15**
(not continuous)
Auckland Quay BN23: Eastb .4G **17**
Austen Wlk. BN23: Lang .3D **16**
Avard Cres. BN20: Eastb .1D **18**
Avenue, The BN21: Eastb .2D **2** (4H **19**)
BN27: Hails .3D **6**
Avenue Ct. BN21: Eastb .1D **2**
Avenue La. BN21: Eastb .1D **2** (4H **19**)
Avenue Mans. BN21: Eastb .3G **3**
Avenue M. BN21: Eastb .1D **2**
Avenue Pl. BN21: Eastb .1D **2**
Avocet BN27: Hails .2C **6**
Avon Ct. BN23: Lang .2C **16**
Avondale Rd. BN22: Eastb .3B **20**
Avonmore BN20: Eastb .6C **2** (1G **23**)
Aylesbury Av. BN23: Eastb .5E **17**
Ayscue Cl. BN23: Eastb .6F **17**
Ayscue Ct. BN23: Eastb .6F **17**

B

Babylon Track BN20: Jev, Will .5A **14**
Babylon Way BN20: Will .5D **14**
Badgers Brow BN20: Will .5D **14**
Badlesmere Rd. BN22: Eastb .1A **20**
Bahram Rd. BN26: Pole .5B **8**
Bailey Cres. BN22: Will .2D **14**
Baillie Av. BN22: Eastb .2C **20**
Bakers Farm Pk. Homes BN27: Hails .4C **4**
Bakers Rd. BN21: Eastb .1A **2** (4F **19**)
Bakewell Rd. BN21: Eastb .3F **19**
Baldwin Av. BN21: Eastb .1E **19**
Bannatyne's Health Club Eastbourne .4A **16**
Banner Way BN24: Sto C .5B **10**
Barbuda Quay BN23: Eastb .6G **17**
Barchester Pl. BN21: Eastb .4E **3**
Barcombe Cl. BN20: Eastb .4E **19**
Barcombe Wlk. BN20: Eastb .4E **19**
Barden Rd. BN22: Eastb .3C **20**
Barming Cl. BN23: Lang .3D **16**
Barn Cl. BN24: Sto C .5A **10**
BN27: Hails .6E **5**
Barnham Cl. BN22: Eastb .3A **16**
Barons Way BN26: Pole .6B **8**
Barrie Cl. BN23: Lang .3E **17**
Barrier Reef Way BN23: Eastb .3G **17**
Bartley Mill Cl. BN24: Sto C .6B **10**
Baslow Rd. BN20: Eastb .2F **23**
Batesman Ho. BN22: Eastb .1D **20**
Bathford Cl. BN23: Lang .3D **16**
Bath Rd. BN21: Eastb .3D **2** (5H **19**)
Battle Cres. BN27: Hails .1D **6**
Battle Rd. BN27: Hails .1D **6**
Bay Av. BN24: Pev B .4C **12**
Bay Cotts. BN24: Nor B .2G **13**
Bayham Rd. BN22: Eastb .1H **3** (3C **20**)
BN27: Hails .2F **7**
Bay Pond Rd. BN21: Eastb .3F **19**
Bay Rd. BN24: Pev B .5B **12**
Bay Ter. *BN24: Pev B .4B 12*
(off Marine Ter.)
Bay Tree La. BN26: Pole .3B **8**
Bay Tree La. Link BN26: Pole .3B **8**
Bay Vw. Camping & Caravanning Pk.
BN24: Pev B .3H **17**
Bay View Golf Course .3H **17**
Beachings, The BN24: Pev B .5A **12**
BEACHLANDS .3D **12**
Beachlands Way BN24: Pev B .3D **12**
Beach Rd. BN22: Eastb .2C **20**
Beach Vw. BN22: Eastb .3C **20**
Beachy Head .6E **23**
Beachy Head Countryside Cen. .5D **22**
Beachy Head Rd.
BN20: E Dean, Eastb .6A **22**
Beamsley Hall *BN22: Eastb .3C 20*
(off Beamsley Rd.)
Beamsley Rd. BN22: Eastb .3C **20**
Beatrice La. BN21: Eastb .1C **2** (4H **19**)
Beatty Rd. BN23: Eastb .1E **21**
Beaufort Ct. BN21: Eastb .1E **3** (4A **20**)
Beaulieu Dr. BN24: Sto C .6A **10**
Beckenham Cl. BN27: Hails .4D **4**
Bedford Gro. BN21: Eastb .3H **19**
Bedfordwell Ct. BN22: Eastb .3A **20**
Bedfordwell Rd. BN21: Eastb .3H **19**
Bedfordwell Rdbt. *BN21: Eastb .3A 20*
(off Bedfordwell Rd.)
Beech Ct. *BN26: Pole .5C 8*
(off Walnut Wlk.)
Beechfield Cl. BN24: Sto C .6B **10**
Beechwood Cl. BN27: Hails .4D **6**
Beechwood Cres.
BN20: Eastb .2A **2** (4F **19**)
Beechy Av. BN20: Eastb .3D **18**
Beechy Gdns. BN20: Eastb .3D **18**
Beggar's La. BN24: Sto C .6C **10**
Belfry, The BN27: Hails .1C **6**
Bell Banks Rd. BN27: Hails .2E **7**
Belle Vue Ct. *BN22: Eastb .2C 20*
(off Belle Vue Rd.)
Belle Vue Rd. BN22: Eastb .2C **20**
Belmont Ct. BN27: Hails .2D **6**
Belmore Rd. BN22: Eastb .1H **3** (3B **20**)
Beltring Rd. BN22: Eastb .3B **20**
Beltring Ter. BN22: Eastb .3B **20**
Beltry Ct. BN21: Eastb .3F **3**
Belvedere BN23: Eastb .4G **17**
Belvedere Ct. BN21: Eastb .3H **19**
Bembridge Rd. BN23: Lang .2B **16**
Benbow Av. BN23: Eastb .1E **21**
Benjamin Cl. BN22: Eastb .3H **15**
Beristede Cl. BN20: Eastb .6B **2** (6G **19**)
Berkeley Ct. BN21: Eastb .5E **3**
Berkeley Wlk. BN23: Lang .3E **17**
Berkshire Ct. *BN22: Eastb .3B 20*
(off Leslie St.)
Bermuda Pl. BN23: Eastb .5G **17**
Bernard La. BN21: Eastb .1C **2** (4H **19**)
Bernhard Gdns. BN26: Pole .6B **8**
Berwick Cl. BN22: Eastb .2E **15**
Berwick Ct. BN21: Eastb .1G **3**
Beuzeville Av. BN27: Hails .1D **6**
Beverington Cl. BN21: Eastb .1F **19**
Beverington Rd. BN21: Eastb .1F **19**
Beverley Ct. *BN20: Eastb .1H 23*
(off South Cliff)
Beverley Ho. BN21: Eastb .2G **3** (4B **20**)
Bex Ct. BN21: Eastb .3H **19**
Bexfield Ct. BN20: Eastb .6D **2** (6H **19**)
Bexhill Rd. BN22: Eastb .2C **20**
BN24: Pev .4H **11**
Bexley Cl. BN27: Hails .5D **4**
Biddenden Cl. BN23: Lang .3D **16**
Bilbury M. BN21: Eastb .2H **19**
Bimini Ct. BN23: Eastb .5G **17**
Binsted Cl. BN22: Eastb .3G **15**
Birch Cl. BN23: Eastb .6D **16**
Birch Ind. Est. BN23: Eastb .6C **16**
Birch Rd. BN23: Eastb .6C **16**
Birch Rdbt. BN22: Eastb .6D **16**
Birch Way BN27: Hails .3D **6**
Birling St. BN21: Eastb .3E **19**
Biscay Av. BN23: Eastb .5E **17**
Blackmans Yd. *BN27: Hails .2E 7*
(off Market St.)
BLACKNESS .5A **10**
Black Path BN26: Pole .5C **8**
Blacksmiths Copse BN27: Hails .3C **6**
Blackthorn Cl. BN22: Eastb .3G **15**
Blackwater Rd. BN20: Eastb .5B **2** (6H **19**)
BN21: Eastb .5B **2** (6H **19**)
Blakes Way BN23: Eastb .1F **21**
Blatchington Mill Dr. BN24: Sto C .6B **10**
Blenheim Way BN26: Pole .5F **9**
Blossom Wlk. BN27: Hails .6D **4**
Bodiam Cres. BN22: Eastb .3A **16**
Bodmin Cl. BN20: Eastb .4E **19**
Bolsover Ct. BN20: Eastb .1H **23**
Bolsover Rd. BN20: Eastb .1H **23**
Bolton Rd. BN21: Eastb .3F **3** (5A **20**)
Boniface Cl. BN24: Sto C .5C **10**
Borough La. BN20: Eastb .1A **2** (4F **19**)
Borrowdale Cl. BN23: Lang .1C **16**
Boscawen Cl. BN23: Eastb .6F **17**
Boship Cl. BN23: Lang .1A **16**
Boship Rdbt. BN27: Lwr D .4A **4**
Boston Cl. BN23: Eastb .6F **17**
Boswell Wlk. BN23: Lang .3E **17**
Boulevard, The BN24: Pev B .3C **12**
Bourne M. BN21: Eastb .1F **3**
Bourneside Ct. BN21: Eastb .2H **3** (4B **20**)
Bourne St. BN21: Eastb .1F **3** (4B **20**)
Bowley Rd. BN27: Hails .2E **7**
Bowood Av. BN22: Eastb .1B **20**
Bracken Rd. BN20: Eastb .2C **18**
(not continuous)
Bradford Ct. *BN22: Eastb .3B 20*
(off Firle Rd.)
Bradford St. BN21: Eastb .4E **19**

Brading Cl. BN23: Lang 1B **16**
Bradley Dr. BN27: Hell 2F **5**
Bramber Ho. BN21: Eastb 1A **2**
Bramble Cl. BN23: Lang 2B **16**
Bramble Dr. BN27: Hails 2C **6**
Bramley Rd. BN26: Pole 5E **9**
Brampton Rd. BN22: Eastb 4H **15**
Brampton Rd. Trad. Est.
BN22: Eastb 5H **15**
Brampton Vs. *BN21: Eastb 3G **19***
(off Watts La.)
Brand Rd. BN22: Eastb 4G **15**
Branston Rd. BN22: Eastb 4F **15**
Brassey Av. BN22: Eastb 4G **15**
Brassey Pde. BN22: Eastb 4G **15**
Brede Cl. BN22: Eastb 1D **20**
Brendon Cl. BN23: Lang 1E **17**
Briar Pl. BN23: Lang 2B **16**
Bridge End BN24: Pev 4H **11**
Bridgemere Rd. BN22: Eastb 1A **20**
Brightland Rd.
BN20: Eastb 1A **2** (4F **19**)
Brightling Rd. BN26: Pole 6C **8**
Brisbane Quay BN23: Eastb 3G **17**
Britland Est. BN22: Eastb 1C **20**
Britten Cl. BN23: Lang 2D **16**
Broad Oak Cl. BN23: Lang 1A **16**
Broad Oaks BN20: Eastb 6B **2** (6G **19**)
Broad Rd. BN20: Will 1B **14**
Broadview Cl. BN20: Will 2B **14**
Broadwater M. BN26: Pole 2A **14**
Broadwater Rdbt. BN22: Eastb 5H **15**
Broadwater Way BN22: Eastb 5H **15**
Broadway, The BN22: Eastb 4F **15**
Broadway M. BN22: Eastb 4F **15**
Brocks Ghyll BN20: Will 2C **14**
Brodie Pl. BN21: Eastb 3F **19**
Brodrick Cl. BN22: Eastb 4H **15**
Brodrick Rd. BN22: Eastb 3F **15**
Bromley Cl. BN23: Lang 3C **16**
Brook Ct. BN20: Eastb 6B **2** (6G **19**)
Brookland Cl. BN24: Pev B 3C **12**
Brookmead Cl. BN22: Eastb 2B **20**
Brookside Av. BN26: Pole 4B **8**
Brook St. BN26: Pole 5B **8**
Broom Cl. BN22: Eastb 3F **15**
Broomfield St. BN20: Eastb 3E **19**
BN21: Eastb 3E **19**
Brow, The BN20: Fris 1B **22**
Browning Wlk. *BN23: Lang 3E **17***
(off The Rising)
Brown Jack Av. BN26: Pole 5B **8**
Brunel Dr. BN27: Hails 5B **4**
Brydges Cl. BN22: Eastb 1C **20**
Buckhurst Cl. BN20: Will 5D **14**
Buckle Gdns. BN27: Hell 2E **5**
Burfield Pk. Ind. Est.
BN27: Hails 2C **6**
Burfield Rd. BN22: Eastb 1H **3** (4B **20**)
Burleigh Pl. BN22: Eastb 1C **20**
Burlington Ct. BN21: Eastb 4F **3**
Burlington Mans. BN21: Eastb 4F **3**
Burlington Pl.
BN21: Eastb 4F **3** (5A **20**)
Burlington Rd.
BN21: Eastb 3G **3** (5B **20**)
Burlow Cl. BN22: Eastb 2E **15**
Burnside BN26: Pole 5C **8**
Burnside Ct. BN26: Pole 5C **8**
Burrow Down BN20: Eastb 2D **18**
Burrow Down Cl. BN20: Eastb 2C **18**
Burton Rd. BN21: Eastb 1F **19**
Burton Wlk. *BN27: Hails 2D **6***
(off Lindfield Dr.)
Burwash Cl. BN23: Lang 1B **16**
Busby Ct. BN21: Eastb 2G **3**
Busheyfields BN27: Hails 1C **6**
Buttermere Way BN23: Lang 1C **16**
Butts Fld. BN27: Hails 3E **7**
Butts La. BN20: Will 5B **14**
Buxton Lodge *BN20: Eastb 1G **23***
(off Buxton Rd.)
Buxton Rd. BN20: Eastb 1G **23**
Byland Cl. BN22: Eastb 2G **15**
Byron Wlk. *BN23: Lang 2E **17***
(off The Rising)

C

Cabot Cl. BN23: Eastb 6G **17**
Caburn Cl. BN23: Lang 1A **16**
Caburn Way BN27: Hails 3C **6**
Cacklebury *BN27: Hails 3C **6***
(off The Holt)
Cacklebury Cl. BN27: Hails 3C **6**
Cade St. BN22: Eastb 3H **15**
Cadogan Ct. BN24: Pev B 5A **12**
Cairngorm Cl. BN23: Lang 2D **16**
Callao Quay BN23: Eastb 5G **17**
Calverley Rd. BN21: Eastb 3D **2** (5H **19**)
Calverley Wlk. BN21: Eastb 3D **2**
Camber Cl. BN24: Pev B 3D **12**
Camber Dr. BN24: Pev B 3D **12**
Camber Way BN24: Pev B 3D **12**
Cambridge Rd. BN22: Eastb 3C **20**
Camden Rd. BN21: Eastb 3D **2** (5H **19**)
Cameron Cl. BN27: Hails 1C **6**
Campbell Circuit 2A **14**
Campbell M. BN23: Eastb 4G **17**
Canary Quay BN23: Eastb 5F **17**
Canterbury Cl. BN22: Will 3D **14**
Canute Cl. BN23: Eastb 5F **17**
Capella Path BN27: Hails 2F **7**
Carbury BN20: Eastb 6B **2**
Carew Ct. *BN21: Eastb 3H **19***
(off Carew Rd.)
*BN27: Hails 4E **5***
(off Hawkswood Rd.)
Carew Lodge BN21: Eastb 2H **19**
Carew Rd. BN21: Eastb 3G **19**
Carew Views BN21: Eastb 2H **19**
Carillon Ho. *BN21: Eastb 3H **19***
(off Eversfield Rd.)
Carisbrooke Cl. BN23: Lang 1B **16**
Carlisle Rd. BN20: Eastb 6A **2** (1F **23**)
(not continuous)
BN21: Eastb 5F **3** (6G **19**)
Carlton Rd. BN22: Eastb 2C **20**
Carmen Ct. BN20: Will 2C **14**
Carmine Ct. BN21: Eastb 4F **3**
Caroline Way BN23: Eastb 4H **17**
Carpenters Way BN27: Hails 3C **6**
Carpet Gardens, The 3G **3**
Carriage House, The BN20: Eastb 6C **2**
Carriers Path BN27: Hails 1E **7**
Carroll Ho. BN21: Eastb 3G **19**
Carroll Wlk. BN23: Lang 3E **17**
CARTERS CORNER 1H **5**
Castle Bolton BN23: Lang 1C **16**
Castle Dr. BN24: Pev B 5A **12**
Castle Mt. BN20: Eastb 6F **19**
Castle Rd. BN24: Pev 5G **11**
Castleross Rd. BN24: Pev B 5A **12**
Castle Vw. Caravan & Camping Site
BN24: Pev B 2H **17**
Castle Vw. Gdns. BN24: W'ham 5E **11**
Cator Ho. BN21: Eastb 2G **3** (4B **20**)
Catsfield Cl. BN23: Lang 1A **16**
Cavalry Cres. BN20: Eastb 2D **18**
Cavendish Av. BN22: Eastb 1G **3** (3B **20**)
Cavendish Pl. BN21: Eastb 1F **3** (4A **20**)
Cavendish Sports Cen. 2F **19**
Caxtons M. BN21: Eastb 2F **3** (4A **20**)
Cecil Ct. BN21: Eastb 3D **2** (5H **19**)
Cedar Cl. BN22: Eastb 3F **15**
Cedars, The BN27: Hails 6D **4**
Centauri Ct. BN23: Eastb 5G **17**
Central Av. BN20: Eastb 2D **18**
BN26: Pole 4D **8**
Centre, The BN26: Pole 5C **8**
Ceylon Pl. BN21: Eastb 2G **3** (4B **20**)
BN22: Eastb 2G **3** (4B **20**)
Chaffinch Rd. BN23: Lang 3C **16**
Chailey Cl. BN23: Lang 4E **17**
Chalk Farm Cl. BN20: Will 4D **14**
Chalvington Ho. *BN21: Eastb 3F **19***
(off Ocklynge Rd.)
Chalvington Rd. BN21: Eastb 6E **15**
Chamberlain Rd. BN21: Eastb 3E **19**
Channel Vw. Rd. BN22: Eastb 2C **20**
BN24: Pev B 4C **12**
Chantry, The BN21: Eastb 3G **19**
Chapel Barn Cl. BN27: Hails 2E **7**
Charles Moore Ct. BN26: Pole 4C **8**
Charleston Rd. BN21: Eastb 3E **19**
Chartwell Ho. BN21: Eastb 2D **2**
Chatfield Cres. BN22: Will 4E **15**
Chatham Ct. BN23: Eastb 3H **17**
Chatham Grn. BN23: Eastb 4H **17**
Chatsworth Gdns. BN20: Eastb 1H **23**
Chatsworth Ho. BN21: Eastb 4F **3**
Chatsworth Wlk. BN21: Eastb 3E **3** (5A **20**)
Chaucer Bus. Pk. BN26: Pole 5G **9**
Chaucer Ind. Est. BN26: Pole 5F **9**
Chaucer Wlk. *BN23: Lang 2E **17***
(off Close Seventeen)
Chawbrook M. BN22: Eastb 3B **20**
Chawbrook Rd. BN22: Eastb 3B **20**
Chelmsford Ct. BN20: Eastb 6C **2** (6H **19**)
Chelworth Rd. BN22: Eastb 3F **15**
Cheriton Ct. BN21: Eastb 3E **19**
Cherry Gdn. Rd. BN20: Eastb 4D **18**
Cherry Side BN27: Hails 1C **6**
Cherwell Cl. BN24: Sto C 6H **9**
Cheshire Ct. *BN22: Eastb 3B **20***
(off Leslie St.)
Chesterfield Gdns. BN20: Eastb 1G **23**
Chesterfield Rd. BN20: Eastb 1G **23**
Chestnut Cl. BN22: Eastb 3F **15**
BN27: Hails 6C **4**
Chestnut Dr. BN26: Pole 5C **8**
Cheviot Cl. BN23: Lang 2C **16**
Chichester Cl. BN22: Will 3D **14**
Chichester Rd. BN27: Hell 2E **5**
Chilham Cl. BN23: Lang 3D **16**
Chiltern Cl. BN23: Lang 1D **16**
Chiltern Ct. BN26: Pole 4C **8**
Chiswick Pl. BN21: Eastb 4F **3** (5A **20**)
Chitty Ho. BN23: Eastb 6D **16**
Christchurch Pl. BN23: Eastb 4G **17**
Church, The BN21: Eastb 2G **3** (4B **20**)
Church Acre Drove BN27: Pev, Wart 1F **11**
Church Av. BN24: W'ham 5G **11**
Church Bailey BN24: W'ham 6G **11**
Church Cl. BN20: Will 1C **14**
Churchdale Av. BN22: Eastb 1C **20**
Churchdale Pl. BN22: Eastb 1B **20**
Churchdale Rd. BN22: Eastb 6B **16**
Churchfield BN20: E Dean 3B **22**
Churchfield Sq. BN21: Eastb 4H **3**
Churchill Cl. BN20: Eastb 4F **19**
Churchill Ct. BN21: Eastb 5E **3**
Church La. BN21: Eastb 4F **19**
BN24: Pev 5H **11**
BN27: Hell 1C **4**
Church M. BN20: Will 4D **14**
Church Path BN27: Hell 2C **4**
Church Rd. *BN24: Pev 5H **1***
(off High St.
BN26: Pole 5C **8**
BN27: Hell 2B **4**
Church St. BN20: Will 4D **1**
BN21: Eastb 1A **2** (4F **19**
BN22: Will 3E **1**
Chyngton Cl. BN23: Lang 1A **1**
Cineworld Cinema
Eastbourne 4F **1**
Circus, The BN23: Eastb 5D **1**
City Gym Express 3D
Clandon Ho. BN22: Eastb 1D **2**
Clarence Ct. BN24: Pev B 6A **1**
Clarence Ho. BN20: Eastb 5B
Clarence Rd. BN22: Eastb 3B **2**
Clarendon Ct. *BN20: Eastb 1H **2***
(off Bolsover Rd
Claxton Cl. BN21: Eastb 2F **1**
Clayton Mill Rd. BN24: Sto C 6B **1**
Cleevelands BN22: Will 3D **1**

Clement La. BN26: Pole 6C **8**
Cleveland Cl. BN23: Lang 2C **16**
Cliff Ho. BN20: Eastb 1G **23**
Clifford Av. BN21: Eastb 1E **19**
Clifford Ho. BN21: Eastb 4F **3**
Cliff Rd. BN20: Eastb 2G **23**
Clifton Cl. BN22: Eastb 5F **15**
Clifton Ct. BN21: Eastb 3E **3**
Clifton Ho. BN22: Eastb 5F **15**
Clive Ct. BN21: Eastb 3G **3**
Cloisters, The BN22: Will 3E **15**
Close, The BN20: Fris 2A **22**
BN20: Will 5D **14**
BN22: Eastb 3E **15**
Close Eight BN23: Lang 2E **17**
Close Eighteen BN23: Lang 3E **17**
Close Eleven BN23: Lang 2E **17**
Close Fifteen BN23: Lang 3E **17**
Close Five BN23: Lang 2E **17**
Close Four BN23: Lang 3E **17**
Close Fourteen BN23: Lang 2E **17**
Close Nine BN23: Lang 3E **17**
Close Nineteen BN23: Lang 3E **17**
Close One BN23: Lang 3D **16**
Close Seven BN23: Lang 2E **17**
Close Seventeen BN23: Lang 3E **17**
Close Six BN23: Lang 2E **17**
Close Sixteen BN23: Lang 3E **17**
Close Ten BN23: Lang 3E **17**
Close Three BN23: Lang 3D **16**
Close Twelve BN23: Lang 3E **17**
Close Twenty BN23: Lang 3E **17**
Close Twentyfive BN23: Lang 3D **16**
Close Twentyfour
BN23: Lang 3E **17**
Close Two BN23: Lang 3D **16**
Clovelly BN21: Eastb 4D **2**
Clovelly Ho. BN26: Pole 4B **8**
Clovis Ct. BN21: Eastb 1E **3** (4A **20**)
Clyde Pk. BN27: Hails 2F **7**
Coastguard Cl. BN24: Nor B 1H **13**
Coastguard Cotts. BN24: Nor B 1H **13**
Coastguard Sq. *BN22: Eastb 3C 20*
(off Addingham Rd.)
Coast Rd. BN24: Nor B, Pev B 4B **12**
Cobald Rd. BN24: Pev B 4C **12**
Cobbold Av. BN21: Eastb 1E **19**
Cobden Pl. *BN27: Hails 2D 6*
(off Station Rd.)
Cochrane Cl. BN23: Eastb 6E **17**
Coldthorn La. BN27: Hails 5C **6**
Coleridge Wlk. *BN23: Lang 3E 17*
(off Close Fifteen)
College Ct. BN21: Eastb 4D **2**
College Grn. BN21: Eastb 3G **19**
College Rd. BN21: Eastb 4D **2** (5H **19**)
Collier Cl. BN22: Eastb 6B **16**
Collier Rd. BN24: Pev B 5B **12**
Collington Cl. BN20: Eastb 6B **2** (6G **19**)
Collingwood Cl. BN23: Eastb 1E **21**
Colonel Stevens Ct.
BN20: Eastb 6C **2** (6H **19**)
Colonnade Gdns. BN21: Eastb 2H **3** (4B **20**)
Colonnade Rd. BN21: Eastb 2H **3** (4B **20**)
Coltstocks Rd. BN20: Eastb 1F **23**
Columbus Dr. BN23: Eastb 6F **17**
Colville Ct. *BN21: Eastb 3G 19*
(off Selwyn Rd.)
Colwood Cres. BN20: Eastb 2D **18**
Combe, The BN20: Will 6C **14**
Combe Ri. BN20: Will 3C **14**
Command Rd. BN20: Eastb 2D **18**
Commercial M. Nth.
BN21: Eastb 1F **3** (3A **20**)
Commercial M. Sth.
BN21: Eastb 1E **3** (4A **20**)
Commercial Rd. BN21: Eastb 1E **3** (4A **20**)
Compass Ct. BN21: Eastb 3F **3**
Compass Point BN23: Eastb 6F **17**
Compton Ct. BN21: Eastb 2B **2** (4G **19**)
Compton Dr. BN20: Eastb 5E **19**
Compton Grange BN20: Eastb 6B **2**
Compton Ho. BN21: Eastb 6E **3**
Compton Ind. Est. BN23: Eastb 6D **16**
Compton Lodge BN21: Eastb 3B **2** (4G **19**)
Compton Pl. Rd. BN20: Eastb 1A **2** (4G **19**)
BN21: Eastb 3A **2** (4G **19**)
Compton St. BN21: Eastb 6E **3** (6A **20**)
Compton Ter. BN27: Hails 3E **7**
Condover Ho. BN21: Eastb 4F **3**
Congress Theatre
Eastbourne 5E 3 (6A 20)
Conifers, The BN21: Eastb 3H **19**
Coniston Rd. BN23: Lang 1C **16**
Connaught Rd. BN21: Eastb 3E **3** (5A **20**)
Conquest Dr. BN27: Hails 4F **5**
Constable Rd. BN23: Lang 4D **16**
Cook Av. BN23: Eastb 1E **21**
Coombe Rd. BN20: Eastb 3E **19**
Coopers Cft. BN20: Will 3D **14**
Coopers Hill BN20: Will 3D **14**
Coopers Way BN27: Hails 3C **6**
Cophall La. BN20: E Dean 3C **22**
Coppice Av. BN20: Will 1C **14**
Coppice Cl. BN20: Will 1C **14**
Copthorne Ho. BN21: Eastb 1A **2**
Coral Reef Cl. BN23: Eastb 4G **17**
Cormorant Cl. BN23: Lang 3C **16**
Cornfield Grn. BN27: Hails 6E **5**
Cornfield La. BN21: Eastb 3E **3** (5A **20**)
Cornfield Rd. BN21: Eastb 3E **3** (5A **20**)
Cornfield Ter. BN21: Eastb 3E **3** (5A **20**)
Cornish Cl. BN23: Lang 1B **16**
Cornmill Gdns. BN26: Pole 1A **14**
Cornwall Ct. BN20: Eastb 2E **19**
Cornwallis Cl. BN23: Eastb 6F **17**
Cotswold Cl. BN23: Lang 1C **16**
Cotswold Ct. BN21: Eastb 4E **3**
Cottage La. BN24: Hank 2G **9**
County Court
Eastbourne 3C 2 (5H 19)
Court, The BN20: Will 4D **14**
Courtland BN21: Eastb 4D **2**
Courtland Rd. BN26: Pole 6C **8**
Courtlands Rd. BN22: Eastb 2A **20**
Court Rd. BN22: Eastb 3H **15**
Coventry Ct. *BN22: Eastb 1D 20*
(off Allfrey Rd.)
Cowbeech Hill BN27: Cowb 1H **5**
Cranborne Av. BN20: Eastb 1E **23**
Cranborne Ct. BN21: Eastb 4F **3**
Crawley Cres. BN22: Eastb 3G **15**
Crescent, The BN20: Eastb 2D **18**
BN20: Will 2C **14**
Cresta Cl. BN26: Pole 4C **8**
Croft, The BN20: Will 4D **14**
BN21: Eastb 3H **19**
Croft Cl. BN26: Pole 1B **14**
Croft Ct. BN21: Eastb 1A **2** (3G **19**)
(Moat Cft. Rd.)
BN21: Eastb 1G **3** (4B **20**)
(Thornton Ct.)
Croft Works BN27: Hails 2D **6**
Cromarty Wlk. BN23: Eastb 5F **17**
Cromer Way BN27: Hails 5C **4**
Cross Levels Way BN21: Eastb 1G **19**
BN22: Eastb 1G **19**
BN23: Eastb 5H **15**
Cross St. BN26: Pole 5C **8**
Crossways, The BN24: Sto C 5A **10**
Crouch Cl. BN20: Will 4D **14**
Crowhurst Cl. BN23: Lang 1A **16**
Crowlink La. BN20: Fris 3A **22**
Crown Cl. BN27: Hails 2C **6**
Crowne Ho. BN21: Eastb 1A **2**
Crown St. BN21: Eastb 3F **19**
Croxden Ct. BN22: Eastb 2F **15**
Croxden Way BN22: Eastb 2F **15**
CRUMBLES, THE 4F 17
Crunden Rd. BN20: Eastb 3E **19**
Cuckmere Cl. BN27: Hails 4B **4**
Cuckmere Dr. BN24: Sto C 6A **10**
Cuckmere Ho. BN21: Eastb 1C **2** (4H **19**)
Cuckmere Wlk. BN22: Eastb 4F **15**
Cuckoo Trail 2D 8
Cullenswood Ct. BN20: Eastb 6B **2**
Culver Cl. BN23: Lang 1B **16**
Cumballa Ct. BN20: Eastb 1H **23**
Cumbria Ct. BN23: Lang 2C **16**
Cunningham Dr. BN23: Eastb 6E **17**
Curzon Cinema
Eastbourne 2F 3 (4A 20)

D

Dacre Pk. BN27: Hails 2F **7**
Dacre Rd. BN20: Eastb 4E **19**
BN21: Eastb 4E **19**
Dale Ct. BN20: Eastb 6B **2** (6G **19**)
Dallaway Dr. BN24: Sto C 6B **10**
Dallington Rd. BN22: Eastb 4H **15**
Dalton Rd. BN20: Eastb 1G **23**
Danum Cl. BN27: Hails 4E **5**
Darent Cl. BN24: Sto C 6H **9**
Darley Rd. BN20: Eastb 1F **23**
Darrick Ct. BN21: Eastb 6E **3**
Darwell Dr. BN24: Sto C 6A **10**
David Hgts. BN21: Eastb 2G **19**
David Lloyd Leisure
Eastbourne 5H 15
Dawber Bldgs. BN27: Hails 2D **6**
Daytona Quay BN23: Eastb 5F **17**
Dean Wood Cl. BN23: Lang 1A **16**
Decoy Dr. BN22: Eastb 5F **15**
Decoy Rdbt. BN21: Eastb 5F **15**
Deer Paddock La. BN27: Hails 2D **6**
Delamere Ct. BN21: Eastb 3D **2**
Delavall Wlk. BN23: Eastb 1F **21**
Dene, The BN20: Will 2C **14**
Dene Cl. BN20: E Dean 2B **22**
Dene Ct. BN21: Eastb 3D **2** (5H **19**)
Dene Dr. BN22: Will 4E **15**
Deneside BN20: E Dean 2B **22**
Den Hill BN20: Eastb 3C **18**
Denstone Ho. BN21: Eastb 4D **2** (5H **19**)
Denton Rd. BN20: Eastb 6A **2** (1F **23**)
Dentons, The BN20: Eastb 1F **23**
De Roos Rd. BN21: Eastb 3G **19**
Derry Ct. BN23: Lang 4D **16**
Derwent Cl. BN27: Hails 6C **4**
Derwent Rd. BN20: Eastb 1G **23**
Desmond Rd. BN22: Eastb 2D **20**
Devonshire Lodge *BN22: Eastb 2C 20*
(off Roselands Av.)
Devonshire Mans. BN21: Eastb 5F **3**
Devonshire Pk. Theatre 5E 3 (6A 20)
Devonshire Pl. BN21: Eastb 3F **3** (5A **20**)
De Walden Ct. BN20: Eastb 6A **2** (6G **19**)
De Walden M. BN20: Eastb 1G **23**
Dickens Way BN23: Lang 2E **17**
Dicker, The BN27: Lwr D 4A **4**
Dillingburgh Rd. BN20: Eastb 3E **19**
Diplock Cl. BN26: Pole 5B **8**
Diplocks, The BN27: Hails 2C **6**
Diplocks Bldgs. BN27: Hails 2C **6**
Diplocks Wlk. BN27: Hails 1C **6**
Diplocks Way BN27: Hails 2C **6**
Discovery Ho. BN21: Eastb 2G **3**
Ditchling Cl. BN23: Lang 1H **15**
Ditchling Way BN27: Hails 3D **6**
Dittons Grange BN21: Eastb 2B **2** (4G **19**)
Dittons Rd. BN21: Eastb 2B **2** (4G **19**)
BN24: Sto C 5G **9**
BN26: Pole 5F **9**
Dixon Ct. BN21: Eastb 1D **2**
Dolphin Ct. BN20: Eastb 2G **23**
Dominica Ct. BN23: Eastb 6G **17**
Donegal Ct. *BN23: Lang 4D 16*
(off Pembury Rd.)
Dorchester Ct. *BN21: Eastb 3G 19*
(off Selwyn Rd.)
Dorset Ct. BN21: Eastb 1G **3**
Douglas Cl. BN27: Hails 5D **4**
Dovedale Gdns. BN22: Eastb 3H **15**
Dover Rd. BN26: Pole 4D **8**
DOWNASH 5F 7
Downash Rd. BN27: Down 4F **7**
Downland Cl. BN23: Lang 1C **16**

Downlands Way BN20: E Dean 2B 22
Downs Av. BN20: Eastb 1D 18
Downside Cl. BN20: Eastb 4E 19
Downsmeade BN21: Eastb 1B 2
Downs Rd. BN22: Will 3D 14
Downsvalley Rd. BN20: Will 1C 14
Downs Vw. Cl. BN20: E Dean 2C 22
Downs Vw. La. BN20: E Dean 2C 22
Downsview Rd. BN20: Will 2C 14
Downsview Way BN27: Hails 2D 6
Drake Av. BN23: Eastb 6E 17
Drive, The BN27: Hails 3D 6
BN27: Hell 2E 5
Drockmill Cl. BN26: Pole 5E 9
Dryden Wlk. *BN23: Lang 2E 17*
(off The Rising)
Dudley Rd. BN22: Eastb 3B 20
Duke Bernard Ct. *BN22: Eastb 2C 20*
(off Carlton Rd.)
Duke's Dr. BN20: Eastb 2F 23
Dunbar Dr. BN27: Hails 6C 4
Durham Ct. BN20: Eastb 1D 18
Durrell Cl. BN23: Lang 3F 17
Dursley Rd. BN22: Eastb 1F 3 (3A 20)
Dutchells Way BN22: Eastb 1F 15
Dymchurch Cl. BN26: Pole 4E 9

E

Earlsmead Ct. BN20: Eastb 6C 2 (6H 19)
EASTBOURNE 2F 3 (4A 20)
Eastbourne Arndale Cen.
BN21: Eastb 2E 3 (4A 20)
Eastbourne Av. BN24: Pev B 4B 12
Eastbourne Bandstand 4G 3 (5B 20)
Eastbourne Borough FC 2F 17
Eastbourne Crematorium
BN23: Lang 2D 16
EASTBOURNE DISTRICT GENERAL HOSPITAL 1G 19
Eastbourne Down Golf Course 5D 18
Eastbourne Golfing Pk. 5A 16
Eastbourne Heritage Cen. 5E 3
Eastbourne Indoor Bowls Club 5G 15
Eastbourne Lifeboat Mus. 5F 3 (6A 20)
Eastbourne Miniature Steam Railway Adventure Pk. 6A 16
Eastbourne Pier 3H 3 (5B 20)
Eastbourne Pier Camera Obscura 3H 3
Eastbourne Rd. BN20: E Dean 3B 22
BN20: Will 5B 8
BN24: Pev B 2H 17
BN24: W'ham 1F 17
BN26: Pole, Will 5B 8
Eastbourne Seven Bingo Club 2F 3
Eastbourne Sports Pk. 5G 15
Eastbourne Station (Rail) 2D 2 (4A 20)
East Cl. BN26: Pole 5D 8
EAST DEAN 3B 22
E. Dean Rd.
BN20: E Dean, Eastb 3C 22 & 6A 18
Eastern Av. BN26: Pole 4D 8
Eastwell Pl. BN27: Hails 1D 6
Eaton Ct. BN21: Eastb 3H 19
Ecmod Rd. BN22: Eastb 1C 20
Eden Cl. BN24: Sto C 6A 10
Edensor Rd. BN20: Eastb 2F 23
Edenthorpe Lodge
BN20: Eastb 1H 23
Edgeland Ter. BN22: Eastb 4H 15
Edinburgh Ct. *BN20: Eastb 2E 19*
(off Central Av.)
Edison Rd. BN23: Eastb 4A 16
Edmund Cl. BN23: Eastb 5E 17
Edward Rd. BN23: Eastb 4A 16
Egbert Cl. BN23: Eastb 5E 17
Egerton Ho. BN20: Eastb 1G 23
Elderwood Cl. BN22: Eastb 3F 15
Eldon Rd. BN21: Eastb 2E 19
Elgar Way BN23: Lang 2E 17
Elim Family Centre, The
BN21: Eastb 1C 2
Elizabeth Ct. BN20: Eastb 2E 19
BN26: Pole 5C 8
BN27: Hails 2E 7
Elm Ct. BN21: Eastb 2D 2
BN26: Pole 5C 8
(off Walnut Wlk.)
Elm Grn. BN27: Hails 6D 4
Elm Gro. BN22: Eastb 4H 15
Elms Av. BN21: Eastb 3G 3 (5B 20)
Elmsdown Pl. BN27: Hails 2E 7
Elms Rd. BN21: Eastb 3G 3 (5B 20)
Elmwood *BN21: Eastb 3H 19*
(off Arundel Rd.)
Elmwood Cl. BN23: Lang 1C 16
Elmwood Gdns. BN23: Lang 1C 16
Elsted Cl. BN22: Eastb 3A 16
Elven Cl. BN20: E Dean 2C 22
Elven La. BN20: E Dean 2C 22
Embassy Ct. BN21: Eastb 2H 19
Endcliffe Ct. BN20: Eastb 1G 23
Ensenada Reef BN23: Eastb 4H 17
Enterprise Shop. Cen. BN21: Eastb 2D 2
Enys Ct. BN21: Eastb 3H 19
Enys Rd. BN21: Eastb 1C 2 (4H 19)
Erica Cl. BN23: Lang 3B 16
Eridge Rd. BN21: Eastb 6E 15
Ersham Rd. BN27: Hails 4D 6
Ersham Way BN27: Hails 3D 6
Eshton Rd. BN22: Eastb 2C 20
Eskdale Cl. BN23: Lang 1B 16
ESPERANCE BMI HOSPITAL 3F 3 (5A 20)
Essex Ct. BN20: Eastb 1D 18
Etchingham Rd. BN23: Lang 4E 17
Ethelred Cl. BN23: Eastb 5E 17
Eton M. BN21: Eastb 1E 3 (4A 20)
Eugene Way BN23: Eastb 4H 17
Eversfield Ct. BN21: Eastb 1D 2
Eversfield Ho. BN21: Eastb 1D 2
Eversfield Rd. BN21: Eastb 1E 3 (3H 19)
Eversley Ct. BN21: Eastb 3G 19
Exceat Cl. BN23: Lang 1A 16
Exeter Cl. BN22: Will 3D 14

F

Factory La. BN27: Hails 2B 6
Fairfield Lodge BN20: Eastb 6B 2 (6G 19)
Fairfield Rd. BN20: Eastb 6B 2 (1G 23)
Fairfields Farm Cvn. Pk.
BN24: W'ham 6F 11
Fair Isle Cl. BN23: Eastb 5E 17
Fairisle Cl. BN27: Hails 5C 4
Fairlight Cl. BN26: Pole 5C 8
Fairlight Rd. BN22: Eastb 2C 20
Fairoaks BN26: Pole 5E 9
Fairway Cl. BN20: Eastb 5E 19
Falcon Way BN27: Hails 4D 4
Falmer Cl. BN20: Eastb 6D 14
BN22: Eastb 4F 15
Falmouth Cl. BN23: Eastb 5F 17
Faraday Cl. BN22: Eastb 4H 15
Farlaine Rd. BN21: Eastb 6E 15
Farmlands Av. BN26: Pole 1B 14
Farmlands Cl. BN26: Pole 1C 14
Farmlands Ct. BN26: Pole 1C 14
Farmlands Way BN26: Pole 6B 8
Farmland Way BN27: Hails 6E 5
Farne Cl. BN27: Hails 5B 4
Farnol Ho. BN21: Eastb 3F 19
Farrington Ct. BN21: Eastb 2C 2 (4H 19)
Fastnet Cl. BN23: Eastb 5E 17
Faversham Rd. BN23: Lang 3D 16
Faygate Rd. BN22: Eastb 3G 15
Featherbed La.
BN27: Hails, Hell, Mag D 3G 5
Fennell's Cl. BN21: Eastb 2G 19
Fern Cl. BN23: Lang 2C 16
Fern Grn. BN27: Hails 6D 4
Fiador Ct. BN23: Eastb 5G 17
Fidley Cl. BN23: Eastb 6E 17
Fieldings, The BN21: Eastb 3H 19
Fiennes Cl. BN21: Eastb 3E 19
Fife Ct. BN22: Eastb 3A 16
FILCHING 2A 14
Filching Cl. BN26: Pole 2A 14
Filching Ct. BN20: Eastb 2D 18
Filching Rd. BN20: Eastb 2D 18
Filder Cl. BN22: Eastb 1A 20
(not continuous)
Finistere Av. BN23: Eastb 5E 17
Finmere Cl. BN22: Eastb 1C 20
Finmere Ct. BN22: Eastb 1C 20
Finmere Rd. BN22: Eastb 1C 20
Finmere Rd. Ind. Est. BN22: Eastb 6C 16
Firle Rd. BN22: Eastb 3B 20
Fir Tree Cl. BN27: Hails 6E 5
Firwood Cl. BN22: Eastb 4G 15
Fisher Cl. BN23: Eastb 6F 17
Fitness First
Eastbourne 4F 17
Fitzalan Ho. *BN21: Eastb 3H 19*
(off Arundel Rd.)
Fitzgerald Cl. BN20: Eastb 6C 2 (1G 23)
Fitzmaurice Av. BN22: Eastb 2B 20
Fleming Cl. BN23: Lang 3F 17
Fletcher Cl. BN27: Hails 2E 7
Fletching Rd. BN22: Eastb 3A 16
Flimwell Cl. BN23: Lang 1A 16
Foley Cl. BN23: Eastb 6E 17
Folkington La. BN26: Folk 6A 8
Foords La. BN24: Hank 4B 10
Foredown Cl. BN20: Eastb 5E 19
Forest Vw. BN27: Hails 1C 6
Formula Fun Go-Karts 2E 21
(part of Fort Fun)
Fort Fun 2E 21
Fort La. BN22: Eastb 1D 20
Fort Rd. BN22: Eastb 1D 20
Fountains Cl. BN22: Eastb 2G 15
Foxglove Rd. BN23: Lang 2B 16
Foyle Way BN20: Eastb 3F 23
Framfield Way BN21: Eastb 1F 19
Fraser Av. BN23: Eastb 6E 17
Freeland Ho. BN20: Eastb 6C 2
Freeman Av. BN22: Eastb 4G 15
Frenchgate Cl. BN22: Eastb 3H 15
Frenchgate Rd. BN22: Eastb 3H 15
Freshfield Cl. BN27: Hails 3D 6
Freshford Cl. BN23: Lang 3D 16
Freshwater Sq. BN22: Will 2D 14
Freshway, The BN22: Eastb 2E 15
Fridays, The BN20: E Dean 3B 22
FRIDAY STREET 1C 16
Friday St. BN23: Lang 1B 16
FRISTON 1B 22
Friston Av. BN22: Will 4E 15
Friston Cl. BN20: Fris 2A 22
Friston Downs BN20: Fris 1B 22
Friston Hill BN20: E Dean, Fris 2A 22
Friston Ho. BN21: Eastb 3G 19
Frobisher Cl. BN23: Eastb 6E 17
Fulbourne Ho. BN20: Eastb 5B 2 (6G 19)
Furness Cl. BN21: Eastb 3D 2
Furness Rd. BN20: Eastb 4C 2 (5H 19)
BN21: Eastb 4C 2 (5H 19)

G

Gables Ct. BN21: Eastb 1E 3 (3A 20)
Gages, The BN27: Hails 2F 7
Gainsborough Cres. BN23: Lang 4D 16
Gainsborough La. BN26: Pole 5A 8
Gallows Cl. BN24: W'ham 5E 11
Gallows La. BN24: W'ham 5E 11
Galveston Cl. BN23: Eastb 6F 17
Gannet Ho. BN21: Eastb 3F 3 (5A 20)
Garden Ct. BN21: Eastb 4F 3
Gardens, The BN21: Eastb 3A 20
Gardner Cl. BN23: Eastb 6E 17
Garfield Rd. BN27: Hails 2E 7
Garnet Dr. BN20: Will 6E 15
Gaudick Cl. BN20: Eastb 6A 2 (6G 19)
Gaudick Pl. BN20: Eastb 6A 2 (1G 23)
Gaudick Rd. BN20: Eastb 5A 2 (6F 19)

Geering Pk. BN27: Hails 2F **7**
Geering Rd. BN24: Sto C 6B **10**
Gemma Cl. BN27: Hails 2G **7**
George Mews, The *BN27: Hails* *2E* ***7***
(off George St.)
George Stanley M. BN20: Will 4D **14**
George St. BN27: Hails 2E **7**
Gilbert Rd. BN22: Eastb 3B **20**
Gilberts Dr. BN20: E Dean 4B **22**
Gilbert Way BN27: Hails 4D **6**
Gilda Cres. BN26: Pole 5C **8**
Gildredge Rd. BN21: Eastb 2D **2** (4H **19**)
Glade, The BN27: Hails 3B **6**
Gladstone Cl. BN22: Eastb 4H **15**
Gladstone Ct. BN21: Eastb 3G **3**
Glebe Cl. BN20: Eastb 4F **19**
Glen Cl. BN26: Pole 1B **14**
Glen Cotts. BN26: Pole 2B **14**
Glendale Av. BN21: Eastb 1E **19**
Gleneagles Dr. BN27: Hails 6B **4**
Glenmore M. BN21: Eastb 1E **3** (4A **20**)
Glennys Ind. Est. BN22: Eastb 2C **20**
Glenthorne Ho. BN21: Eastb 1C **2**
Glessing Rd. BN24: Sto C 5B **10**
Gloucester Cl. BN22: Will 3E **15**
Gloucester Ct. BN20: Eastb 5C **2** (6H **19**)
BN23: Lang 4E **17**
Gloucester M. BN21: Eastb 3D **2**
Glynde Av. BN22: Eastb 4G **15**
Glynde Ct. BN20: Eastb 5A **2** (6G **19**)
Glyndley Mnr. Cottage Est.
BN24: Hank 1H **9**
Glynleigh Dr. BN26: Pole 4E **9**
Glynleigh Rd. BN24: Hails, Hank 1E **9**
Goffs, The BN21: Eastb 1A **2** (4G **19**)
Golden Ga. M. *BN23: Eastb* *4H* ***17***
(off Golden Ga. Way)
Golden Ga. Way BN23: Eastb 4G **17**
Golden Jubilee Way
BN22: Eastb, Sto C 5G **9**
BN23: Eastb 5G **9**
BN24: Sto C 5G **9**
Golden Miller La. BN26: Pole 5A **8**
Golding Rd. BN23: Lang 3F **17**
Goldring Av. BN27: Hell 2E **5**
Goldsmith Cl. BN23: Lang 2E **17**
Goodwin Cl. BN27: Hails 5C **4**
Goodwood Cl. BN20: Will 3D **14**
Gordon Ho. *BN21: Eastb* *3H* ***19***
(off Carew Rd.)
Gordon Rd. BN27: Hails 2D **6**
Gore Farm Cl. BN20: E Dean 3B **22**
Gore Pk. Av. BN21: Eastb 3F **19**
Gore Pk. Rd. BN21: Eastb 3F **19**
Gornay Dr. BN27: Hails 6B **4**
Gorringe Cl. BN20: Will 2C **14**
Gorringe Dr. BN20: Will 2C **14**
Gorringe Rd. BN21: Eastb 2H **19**
BN22: Eastb 2H **19**
Gorringe Valley Rd. BN20: Will 2C **14**
Gorse Cl. BN20: Eastb 2D **18**
Gosford Way BN26: Pole 5B **8**
Goudhurst Cl. BN23: Lang 4D **16**
Grafton Ct. BN21: Eastb 2G **3** (4B **20**)
Grampian Cl. BN23: Lang 2C **16**
Granary Rural Bus. Centre, The
BN27: Hell 1B **4**
Grand Ct. BN21: Eastb 5F **3** (6A **20**)
Grand Hotel Bldgs.
BN21: Eastb 6E **3** (6A **20**)
Grand Mans. BN20: Eastb 6E **3**
Grand Pde. BN21: Eastb 5F **3** (6A **20**)
BN26: Pole 5B **8**
Grange Ct. BN21: Eastb 4C **2** (5H **19**)
Grange End BN21: Eastb 6D **2** (6H **19**)
Grange Gdns. BN20: Eastb 4C **2**
(Blackwater Rd.)
BN20: Eastb 4C **2** (5H **19**)
(Furness Rd.)
Grange Lodge BN20: Eastb 4C **2**
Grange M. BN21: Eastb 3D **2** (5H **19**)
Grange Rd. BN21: Eastb 3D **2** (5H **19**)
Granville Ct. BN20: Eastb 5C **2** (6H **19**)
Granville Crest BN20: Eastb 1G **23**
Granville Rd. BN20: Eastb 4C **2** (5H **19**)
Grasmere Cl. BN23: Lang 1B **16**
Grassington Rd. BN20: Eastb 4C **2** (5H **19**)
Gt. Cliffe Rd. BN23: Lang 4E **17**
Green, The BN20: E Dean 3B **22**
BN27: Hails 4E **5**
Greenacres Dr. BN27: Hails 1E **7**
Greenacres Way BN27: Hails 1E **7**
Greencroft BN21: Eastb 3G **3**
Greenfield Rd. BN21: Eastb 3F **19**
Greenfields BN27: Hails 6C **4**
Green Gro. BN27: Hails 1D **6**
Greenleaf Gdns. BN26: Pole 3C **8**
Green St. BN21: Eastb 3E **19**
Green Wlk. BN27: Hails 6E **5**
Green Walk, The BN22: Will 2D **14**
Greenway BN20: Eastb 1D **18**
Greenwich Ho. BN20: Eastb 1G **23**
Greenwich Rd. BN27: Hails 2F **7**
Gregory La. BN24: W'ham 6F **11**
Grenada Cl. BN23: Eastb 6G **17**
Grenville Rd. BN24: Pev B 5A **12**
Gresham BN24: Pev 5H **11**
Gresham Cl. BN21: Eastb 1E **19**
Gresham Ho. BN21: Eastb 4G **3** (5B **20**)
Greys Rd. BN20: Eastb 1A **2** (4F **19**)
Grey Twr. Caravan Site BN24: Pev B . . .2H **17**
Grey Tower Rd. BN24: Pev B 2H **17**
Grey Towers Bungs. BN24: Pev B 6A **12**
Groombridge Av. BN22: Eastb 1D **20**
Groombridge Wlk. *BN22: Eastb* *1D* ***20***
(off Groombridge Av.)
Grosvenor Cl. BN26: Pole 6B **8**
Grosvenor Ct. *BN21: Eastb* *3H* ***19***
(off Enys Rd.)
Grove, The BN20: Will 2B **14**
(The Paragon)
BN20: Will .6D **14**
(Up. Ratton Dr.)
BN27: Hails 3D **6**
Grove Hill BN27: Hell 2E **5**
Grovelands Rd. BN27: Hails 6C **4**
Grove Rd. BN21: Eastb 3C **2** (5H **19**)
Guardian Ct. BN26: Pole 4B **8**
Guestling Rd. BN22: Eastb 2D **20**
Gwent Ct. *BN22: Eastb* *3C* ***20***
(off St James Rd.)

H

Hadley Ct. BN26: Pole 6C **8**
Hadley Ho. BN21: Eastb 1D **2** (4H **19**)
Hadlow Av. BN23: Lang 1A **16**
HAILSHAM **1E 7**
Hailsham Heritage Cen. ***2E 7***
(off Market St.)
Hailsham Ind. Pk. BN27: Hails 2C **6**
Hailsham Leisure Cen. **1E 7**
Hailsham Rd. BN24: Hank, Sto C 2G **9**
BN26: Pole 4B **8**
BN27: Hails, Herst, Mag D 4F **5**
Halland Cl. BN22: Will 5F **15**
Halley Pk. BN27: Hails 2F **7**
Halton Rd. BN22: Eastb 3C **20**
Hamble Rd. BN24: Sto C 6H **9**
Hambleton Cl. BN23: Lang 2D **16**
Hamelsham Ct. BN27: Hails 1C **6**
Hamilton Ho. BN21: Eastb 3G **19**
Hamilton Quay BN23: Eastb 5G **17**
Hamlands La. BN22: Will 2D **14**
Hamlins Pk. Cl. BN27: Hails 2F **7**
Hammonds Dr. BN23: Eastb 6C **16**
Hammonds Ind. Est. BN23: Eastb 6B **16**
Hampden Av. BN22: Eastb 4H **15**
Hampden Ct. BN21: Eastb 5E **3**
HAMPDEN PARK **4H 15**
Hampden Pk. Dr. BN22: Eastb 5F **15**
Hampden Pk. Ind. Est. BN22: Eastb 5A **16**
Hampden Pk. Sports Cen. **3G 15**
Hampden Park Station (Rail) **4H 15**
Hampden Retail Pk. BN22: Eastb 4H **15**
Hampden Ter. BN22: Eastb 1H **3**
Hampshire Ct. BN23: Lang 4E **17**
Hampton Ho. *BN27: Hails* *2D* ***6***
(off Summerheath Rd.)
Hamsey Cl. BN20: Eastb 1D **18**
Ham Shaw Ct. BN22: Eastb 5H **15**
HANKHAM **3B 10**
Hankham Ct. BN24: Sto C 6A **10**
Hankham Hall Rd.
BN24: Hank, W'ham 3B **10**
Hankham Rd. BN24: Hank 5B **10**
Hankham St. BN24: Hank 4B **10**
Hanover Ct. BN21: Eastb 2F **19**
BN27: Hails *1E* ***7***
(off St Mary's Av.)
Hanover Rd. BN22: Eastb 3C **20**
Harbour Club Apartments
BN23: Eastb 4G **17**
Harbour Quay BN23: Eastb 4G **17**
Harbour Rdbt. BN23: Eastb 4F **17**
Harding Av. BN22: Eastb 1B **20**
Hardwick Rd. BN21: Eastb 3E **3** (5A **20**)
Hardy Dr. BN23: Eastb 1F **21**
Harebeating Cl. BN27: Hails 5E **5**
Harebeating Cres. BN27: Hails 5E **5**
Harebeating Dr. BN27: Hails 4D **4**
Harebeating Gdns. BN27: Hails 5E **5**
Harebeating La. BN27: Hails 5E **5**
Harebell Cl. BN23: Lang 2C **16**
Harford Battersby Ho.
BN21: Eastb 3F **3**
Hargreaves Bus. Pk. BN23: Eastb 4A **16**
Hargreaves Rd. BN23: Eastb 4A **16**
Harmers Hay Rd. BN27: Hails 5D **4**
Harold Cl. BN24: Pev B 3D **12**
Harold Dr. BN23: Eastb 5E **17**
Harris Ct. BN21: Eastb 2F **3** (4B **20**)
Hartfield La. BN21: Eastb 1D **2** (3H **19**)
Hartfield Rd. BN21: Eastb 1C **2** (4H **19**)
Hartington Mans. BN21: Eastb 3F **3**
Hartington Pl. BN21: Eastb 3F **3** (5A **20**)
Harwood Cl. BN23: Eastb 6E **17**
Hassocks Cl. BN23: Lang 1H **15**
Hastings Cl. BN26: Pole 4D **8**
Hastings Cres. BN27: Hails 5F **5**
Haughton Ho. BN21: Eastb 2G **3**
Havana Ct. BN23: Eastb 5F **17**
Havelock Rd. BN22: Eastb 3B **20**
Haven, The BN27: Hails 3E **7**
Haven Cl. BN22: Will 2D **14**
BN24: Pev B 3C **12**
Hawkhurst Cl. BN23: Lang 3C **16**
Hawkins Way BN27: Hails 1D **6**
Hawksbridge Cl. BN22: Will 2D **14**
Hawks Farm Cl. BN27: Hails 5D **4**
Hawks Rd. BN27: Hails 6D **4**
Hawkstown Cl. BN27: Hails 4D **4**
Hawks Town Cres. BN27: Hails 5D **4**
Hawkstown Gdns. BN27: Hails 4D **4**
Hawkstown Vw. BN27: Hails 4D **4**
Hawkswood Dr. BN27: Hails 4E **5**
Hawkswood Rd. BN27: Hails 4D **4**
Hawthorn Ct. BN26: Pole 5C **8**
Hawthorn Rd. BN23: Eastb 5C **16**
Hawthorn Rd. Ind. Est. BN23: Eastb 5C **16**
Hawthorns, The BN27: Hails 2C **6**
Hawthylands Cres. BN27: Hails 5D **4**
Hawthylands Dr. BN27: Hails 5D **4**
Hawthylands Rd. BN27: Hails 5D **4**
Hayland Grn. BN27: Hails 6E **5**
Haystoun Cl. BN22: Will 3E **15**
Haystoun Pk. BN22: Will 3E **15**
Hazel Gro. BN20: Will 2C **14**
Hazelwood Av. BN22: Eastb 2F **15**
Heather Cl. BN23: Lang 2B **16**
Hebrides Wlk. BN23: Eastb 6E **17**
Hedley Way BN27: Hails 5B **4**
Helen Garden **2G 23**
HELLINGLY **2C 4**
Helvellyn Dr. BN23: Lang 1C **16**
Hempstead La. BN27: Hails 1A **6**
Henfield Rd. BN22: Eastb 3G **15**
Hengist Cl. BN23: Eastb 5E **17**

Henleaze BN21: Eastb 1B 2 (4G 19)
Hereford Ct. BN23: Lang 4E 17
Hereward Rd. BN23: Eastb 4F 17
Heron Cl. BN23: Lang 3C 16
Heron Ridge BN26: Pole 5D 8
Hever Cl. BN23: Lang 3D 16
Hickling Cl. BN23: Lang 1B 16
Hide Hollow BN23: Lang 2D 16
BN24: Lang, W'ham 2E 17
Hide Hollow Roundabouts
BN23: Lang 2C 16
High Cl. BN20: E Dean 1C 22
Highcombe BN20: Eastb 2F 23
Highfield Ind. Est. BN23: Eastb 4A 16
Highfield Link BN23: Eastb 5A 16
Highland Ho. BN21: Eastb 3H 19
Highland Lodge BN21: Eastb 3H 19
Highmead Mnr. BN20: Eastb 1G 23
High St. BN21: Eastb 1A 2 (4F 19)
BN24: Pev, W'ham 6F 11
(not continuous)
BN26: Pole 5C 8
BN27: Hails 1D 6
High Trees BN21: Eastb 3H 19
Highview Ct. BN20: Eastb 6D 2 (6H 19)
Hilary Cl. BN26: Pole 6B 8
Hill Ct. BN20: Eastb 6D 2
Hill Rd. BN20: Eastb 2C 18
Hillside BN20: E Dean 2B 22
Hoad Rd. BN22: Eastb 3B 20
Hobart Quay BN23: Eastb 3G 17
Hobney Ri. BN24: W'ham 6F 11
Hockington La. BN20: Will 4D 14
Hodcombe Cl. BN23: Lang 1B 16
Hogarth Rd. BN23: Lang 4D 16
Holbrook Cl. BN20: Eastb 1G 23
Hollamby Pk. BN27: Hails 2F 7
Holly Cl. BN27: Hails 3D 6
Holly Pl. BN22: Eastb 2G 15
Holt, The BN27: Hails 3C 6
Holyhead Cl. BN27: Hails 6C 4
Holywell Cl. BN20: Eastb 2G 23
Holywell Rd. BN20: Eastb 2G 23
Holywell Wlk. *BN27: Hails* *2D 6*
(off Lindfield Dr.)
Homegate Ho. BN21: Eastb 1D 2 (4H 19)
Homeglade Ho. BN20: Eastb 1G 23
Homelatch Ho. BN21: Eastb 1E 3
Homewood Cl. BN22: Eastb 1B 20
Honeycrag Cl. BN26: Pole 4B 8
Honeysuckle Cl. BN23: Lang 2B 16
BN27: Hails 4D 6
Honeyway Cl. BN26: Pole 2B 14
Hood Cl. BN23: Eastb 6E 17
Hoo Gdns. BN20: Will 4D 14
Horning Cl. BN23: Lang 1B 16
Horsa Cl. BN23: Eastb 5E 17
Horselunges Ind. Est.
BN27: Hell 2D 4
Horsye Rd. BN22: Eastb 6B 16
Houghton Way BN27: Hell 2F 5
Howard Cl. BN27: Hails 3F 7
Howard Ho. BN21: Eastb 5F 3 (5A 20)
Howard Sq. BN21: Eastb 4F 3 (5A 20)
Howe M. BN21: Eastb 1E 3 (4A 20)
Howland Cl. BN23: Eastb 4G 17
Howlett Dr. BN27: Hails 5D 4
Howletts Cl. BN22: Eastb 4H 15
'How We Lived Then' (Museum of Shops)
4E 3
Hudson Cl. BN23: Eastb 6G 17
Hudson Ct. *BN22: Eastb* *1C 20*
(off Churchdale Rd.)
Hudson Ho. BN21: Eastb 3A 20
Huggetts La. BN22: Eastb, Will 3D 14
Hunloke Av. BN22: Eastb 1B 20
Hurst La. BN21: Eastb 3F 19
Hurst Rd. BN21: Eastb 2F 19
Hyde Gdns. BN21: Eastb 3E 3 (5A 20)
Hyde Rd. BN21: Eastb 3D 2 (5H 19)
Hyde Tynings Cl. BN20: Eastb 1E 23
Hydneye, The BN22: Eastb 4H 15
Hydney St. BN22: Eastb 2C 20
Hyperion Av. BN26: Pole 5A 8
Hythe Cl. BN26: Pole 4E 9

I

Iden St. BN22: Eastb 3A 16
Ifield Mill Cl. BN24: Sto C 6B 10
Ilex Grn. BN27: Hails 6D 4
Ingrams Way BN27: Hails 4C 6
Innings Dr. BN24: Pev B 5A 12
International Lawn Tennis Cen.
4E 3 (5A 20)
Iona Cl. BN27: Hails 4C 4
Italian Gdns. 2G 23
Ivy Ter. BN21: Eastb 2D 2 (4H 19)

J

Jack O'Dandy Cl. BN21: Eastb 6E 15
Jamaica Way BN23: Eastb 5F 17
James Caird Ho. BN21: Eastb 2G 3
Jasmine Grn. BN27: Hails 6D 4
Jay Cl. BN23: Lang 3C 16
Jellicoe Cl. BN23: Eastb 6F 17
Jephson Cl. BN20: Eastb 1H 23
Jerome Cl. BN23: Lang 3E 17
Jervis Av. BN23: Eastb 1E 21
Jevington Ct. BN20: Eastb 5A 2 (6G 19)
Jevington Gdns. BN21: Eastb 6D 2 (6H 19)
Jevington Ho. *BN21: Eastb* *3F 19*
(off Upperton Rd.)
Jevington Rd. BN20: Fris 2A 22
BN26: Filch, Jev, Pole 3A 14
Joan Hughes Ct. BN26: Pole 5C 8
Johnston Pl. BN23: Eastb 4G 17
Jordans La. BN22: Eastb 2E 15
Jordans La. E. BN22: Eastb 2F 15
Jordans La. W. BN22: Eastb 2E 15
Jubilee Ho. *BN22: Eastb* *3B 20*
(off Waterworks Rd.)
Junction Rd. BN21: Eastb 2E 3 (4A 20)
Junction St. BN26: Pole 5D 8

K

Keats Wlk. *BN23: Lang* *2E 17*
(off Close Eleven)
Keith Wlk. BN23: Eastb 1F 21
Kennett Cl. BN24: Sto C 6H 9
Kensington BN23: Eastb 4G 17
Kent Ct. BN20: Eastb 1D 18
Kent Ho. BN20: Eastb 1G 23
Kenton Ct. BN21: Eastb 6E 3
Kepplestone BN20: Eastb 1G 23
Kerrara Ter. BN22: Eastb 2B 20
Kerry Ct. BN23: Lang 4D 16
Keymer Cl. BN23: Lang 4E 17
Keymer Ho. BN21: Eastb 1A 2
Key West BN23: Eastb 6F 17
Kilburn Ter. BN21: Eastb 1E 3 (4A 20)
Kildare Ct. BN20: Eastb 4E 19
Kilda St. BN22: Eastb 3B 20
Kilpatrick Cl. BN23: Lang 2D 16
Kinfauns Av. BN22: Eastb 1B 20
King Edwards Pde.
BN20: Eastb 6E 3 (2G 23)
BN21: Eastb 6E 3 (2G 23)
Kingfisher Dr. BN23: Lang 3C 16
King's Av. BN21: Eastb 2G 19
Kings Cl. BN21: Eastb 2G 19
Kings Ct. E. BN23: Eastb 5F 17
Kings Ct. Sth. BN23: Eastb 5F 17
Kings Ct. W. BN23: Eastb 5E 17
King's Dr. BN21: Eastb, Will 5E 15
Kingsford BN23: Eastb 6D 16
Kingsmere Way BN23: Eastb 5E 17
Kings Mt. BN21: Eastb 3G 19
Kings Pk. *BN23: Eastb* *5F 17*
(off Kingsmere Way)
Kingston Ho. BN21: Eastb 1C 2 (3H 19)
Kingston Quay BN23: Eastb 5F 17
Kingston Rd. BN22: Eastb 3H 15
Kingwood Ho. BN21: Eastb 3H 19
Kinross Ct. BN21: Eastb 3A 20
Kipling Wlk. BN23: Lang 3E 17
Kirkstall Cl. BN22: Eastb 2G 15
Kirk Way BN20: Eastb 2D 18
Knights Gdn. BN27: Hails 3D 6
Knockhatch Adventure Pk. 2A 6
Knoll Cres. BN22: Eastb 4H 15
Knoll Rd. BN22: Eastb 3A 16

L

Laburnum Grn. BN27: Hails 6D 4
Laburnum Ho. *BN20: Eastb* *1G 23*
(off Darley Rd.)
Laburnum Wlk. BN22: Eastb 2F 15
Labyrinth, The BN21: Eastb 2E 3
Lakelands Cl. BN22: Eastb 4A 16
Lakeside Ct. BN22: Eastb 4A 16
Laleham Cl. BN21: Eastb 3G 19
Laleham Ct. BN21: Eastb 3G 19
Lambert Rd. BN23: Lang 2E 17
Lambourn Av. BN24: Sto C 6A 10
Lamont Ct. BN21: Eastb 6E 3
Lanark Ct. BN20: Eastb 1D 18
Lancaster Ct. BN22: Eastb 1H 3
Lancing Way BN26: Pole 1B 14
Langdale Cl. BN23: Lang 1C 16
LANGNEY 3C 16
Langney Grn. BN23: Lang 5E 17
Langney Point Roundabouts
BN23: Eastb 6G 17
Langney Ri. BN23: Lang 3D 16
Langney Rd. BN21: Eastb 2F 3 (4A 20)
BN22: Eastb 2G 3 (4B 20)
Langney Rdbt. BN23: Eastb 5E 17
Langney Shop. Cen. BN23: Lang 3C 16
Langney Sports Club 2F 17
LANGNEY VILLAGE 4E 17
Lansdowne Ct. BN21: Eastb 5E 3
Lansdowne Cres. BN27: Hails 5C 4
Lansdowne Dr. BN27: Hails 4C 4
Lansdowne Gdns. BN27: Hails 5D 4
Lansdowne Rd. BN27: Hails 5D 4
Lansdowne Ter. *BN21: Eastb* *6E 3*
(off King Edwards Pde.)
Lansdowne Way BN27: Hails 4C 4
Lapwing Bus. Pk. BN24: Pev 2A 12
Lapwing Cl. BN23: Lang 3C 16
Larch Gdns. BN22: Eastb 2F 15
Larkspur Dr. BN23: Lang 1A 16
La Ronde Ct. BN21: Eastb 3F 3
Lascelles Mans. BN21: Eastb 5F 3
Lascelles Ter. BN21: Eastb 5F 3 (6A 20)
La Serena Pl. BN23: Eastb 4H 17
Latimer Ct. *BN22: Eastb* *3C 20*
(off Latimer Rd.)
Latimer Rd. BN22: Eastb 1H 3 (4C 20)
Laughton Cl. BN23: Lang 1A 16
Lavant Rd. BN24: Sto C 6B 10
Lavender Cl. BN23: Lang 2B 16
BN27: Hails 6B 4
Lawns, The BN20: Will 4D 14
BN22: Eastb 2C 20
BN22: Will 3D 14
BN27: Hails 3E 7
Lawns Av. BN21: Eastb 1A 2 (3F 19)
Lawrence Cl. BN23: Lang 4D 16
Leaf Glen BN21: Eastb 1B 2
Leaf Hall Rd. BN22: Eastb 1H 3 (4B 20)
Leaf Rd. BN21: Eastb 1F 3 (4A 20)
Lea Ho. BN21: Eastb 3G 19
Leahurst BN20: Eastb 6B 2
Leamland Wlk. *BN27: Hails* *2D 6*
(off Lindfield Dr.)
Leap Cross Small Bus. Cen.
BN27: Hails 6C 4
Le Brun Rd. BN21: Eastb 2G 19
Leeds Av. BN23: Eastb 5D 16
Leeward Quay BN23: Eastb 5F 17

Leicester Ct. *BN22: Eastb* *3B* ***20***
(off Leslie St.)
Lennox Cl. BN20: Eastb 2D **18**
Lepeland BN27: Hails 6C **4**
Leslie St. BN22: Eastb 3B **20**
Letheren Pl. BN21: Eastb 4F **19**
Levett Av. BN26: Pole 4E **9**
Levett Cl. BN26: Pole 5E **9**
Levett Rd. BN26: Pole 5E **9**
Levett Way BN26: Pole 5E **9**
Lewes Ct. BN21: Eastb 3A **20**
Lewes Ho. *BN21: Eastb* *3H* ***19***
(off Lewes Rd.)
Lewes Rd. BN21: Eastb 2H **19**
BN26: Folk, Pole 5A **8**
BN26: Pole 5B **8**
Leyland Rd. BN24: Pev B 5B **12**
Lilac Cl. BN22: Eastb 3F **15**
Limes, The BN21: Eastb 1B **2** (3G **19**)
Limetree Av. BN22: Eastb 2F **15**
Lincoln Cl. BN20: Eastb 1E **23**
Lincoln Ct. BN20: Eastb 6D **14**
Linden Cl. BN22: Eastb 2G **15**
Linden Gro. BN27: Hails 4E **5**
Lindfield Dr. BN27: Hails 2D **6**
Lindfield Rd. BN22: Eastb 3F **15**
Lindon Cl. BN20: Fris 2B **22**
Lindsay Cl. BN20: Eastb 5E **19**
Link, The BN20: E Dean 1C **22**
Link Rd. BN20: Eastb 6F **19**
Linkswood BN21: Eastb 3A **2** (5G **19**)
Linkway BN20: Will 6D **14**
Linkway, The BN24: W'ham 5E **11**
Linnet Cl. BN23: Lang 3C **16**
Linosa Ct. BN22: Eastb 1H **3**
Lion Hill BN24: Sto C 6B **10**
Lion Ho. Pk. BN27: Hails 3G **7**
Lion La. BN21: Eastb 2H **3** (4B **20**)
Lismore Rd. BN21: Eastb 3F **3** (5A **20**)
Lister Rd. BN23: Eastb 4A **16**
Littlecote BN20: Eastb 5C **2** (6H **19**)
Lloyds Lane (Ten Pin Bowling) **5G 15**
Lodge, The BN21: Eastb 4E **3** (5A **20**)
Lodge Av. BN22: Will 3E **15**
London Ho. *BN21: Eastb* *3E* ***3***
(off Cornfield Ter.)
London Rd. BN27: Hails 4C **4**
Long Acre Cl. BN21: Eastb 2F **19**
Long Beach Cl. BN23: Eastb 4H **17**
Long Beach M. BN23: Eastb 4H **17**
Long Beach Vw. BN23: Eastb 4H **17**
Longford Ct. BN23: Lang 3D **16**
Longland Rd. BN20: Eastb 3D **18**
Longstone Rd.
BN21: Eastb 2F **3** (4A **20**)
BN22: Eastb 2F **3** (4B **20**)
Lordslaine Cl. BN20: Eastb 1E **23**
Lothian Ct. BN22: Eastb 3H **15**
Lottbridge Dr. BN22: Eastb 3H **15**
Lottbridge Drove BN22: Eastb 6D **16**
BN23: Eastb 4H **15**
Lottbridge Rdbt. BN23: Eastb 5A **16**
Love La. BN20: Eastb 2A **2** (4F **19**)
Lovell Ct. BN21: Eastb 2F **19**
LOWER HORSEBRIDGE **3B 4**
Lower Pde. BN21: Eastb 5F **3** (6A **20**)
Lower Rd. BN21: Eastb 3F **19**
Lower St. BN20: E Dean 3B **22**
LOWER WILLINGDON **2D 14**
Lowlands, The BN27: Hails 6C **4**
Lowther Cl. BN23: Lang 2D **16**
Loxwood Cl. BN22: Will 5E **15**
Luke Lade Ct. *BN27: Hails* *2E* ***7***
(off Bayham Rd.)
Lullington Cl. BN21: Eastb 6E **15**
Lullington Ho. BN21: Eastb 3G **19**
Lundy Wlk. BN23: Eastb 5F **17**
BN27: Hails 4B **4**
Luscombe Av. BN27: Hell 2F **5**
Lushington La. BN21: Eastb 3E **3** (5A **20**)
Lushington Rd. BN21:
Eastb .3E **3** (5A **20**)
Luton Cl. BN21: Eastb 1E **19**
Lydd Cl. BN23: Lang 3D **16**
Lynholm Rd. BN26: Pole 5D **8**

M

Macmillan Dr. BN21: Eastb 2E **19**
Macquarie Quay BN23: Eastb 5G **17**
Madeira Way BN23: Eastb 5F **17**
Magdalen Cl. BN23: Lang 2C **16**
Magellan Way BN23: Eastb 1G **21**
MAGHAM DOWN **3H 5**
Magistrates' Court
Eastbourne . . . .**3C 2 (5H 19)**
Magnolia Dr. BN22: Eastb 3F **15**
Magnolia Wlk. BN22: Eastb 3F **15**
Magpie Rd. BN23: Lang 2C **16**
Mahwood Ho. *BN21: Eastb* *3A* ***20***
(off Bedfordwell Rd.)
Malcolm Ct. BN21: Eastb 3A **20**
Malcolm Gdns. BN26: Pole 4C **8**
Mallard Cl. BN22: Eastb 4H **15**
Malthouse Cotts. *BN20: Will* *4D* ***14***
(off Wish Hill)
Malthouse Way BN27: Hell 2E **5**
Malvern Cl. BN22: Eastb 2F **15**
Manifold Rd. BN22: Eastb 3B **20**
Mannington Rd. BN27: Hell 2F **5**
Manor Cl. BN20: Will 3C **14**
Manor Mobile Home Park, The
BN27: Hell 3E **5**
Manor Pk. Cl. BN27: Hails 4C **4**
Manor Pk. Ct. BN26: Pole 5C **8**
Manor Pk. Rd. BN27: Hails 4C **4**
Manor Rd. BN22: Eastb 3A **16**
Manor Way BN20: Will 5D **14**
BN26: Pole 5C **8**
Mansions, The
BN21: Eastb 5F **3**
Manton Ct. BN23: Eastb 5D **16**
Manvers Rd. BN20: Eastb 4D **18**
Maple Ct. BN27: Hails 1C **6**
Maplehurst Rd. BN22: Eastb 3F **15**
Mapleleaf Gdns. BN26: Pole 3C **8**
Maple Rd. BN23: Eastb 6D **16**
Marcia Cl. BN20: Will 5C **14**
Maresfield Dr. BN24: Pev B 3C **12**
Marina Wlk. BN23: Eastb 5E **17**
Marine Av. BN24: Pev B 3D **12**
Marine Cl. BN24: Pev B 3D **12**
Marine Ct. *BN24: Pev B* *4B* ***12***
(off The Parade)
Marine Gdns. BN21: Eastb 3H **3**
Marine Pde. BN21: Eastb 3H **3** (5B **20**)
BN22: Eastb 2H **3** (4B **20**)
Marine Rd. BN22: Eastb 1H **3** (4B **20**)
BN24: Pev B 4B **12**
Marine Ter. BN24: Pev B 4B **12**
Market Pl. BN27: Hails 2E **7**
Market Sq. BN27: Hails 2E **7**
Market St. BN27: Hails 2E **7**
Mark La. BN21: Eastb 3E **3** (5A **20**)
Marlborough Cl. BN23: Lang 2D **16**
Marlborough Ct.
BN21: Eastb 2C **2**
Marlow Av. BN22: Eastb 1B **20**
Marlow Dr. BN27: Hails 4D **4**
Marsden Rd. BN23: Lang 4E **17**
Marshall Ct. BN22: Eastb 3F **15**
Marshall Rd. BN22: Eastb 5H **15**
BN23: Eastb 5H **15**
Marshall Rdbt. BN23: Eastb 5A **16**
Marshfoot La. BN27: Hails 1E **7**
Marsh Rd. BN24: Pev 2A **12**
BN27: Pev 2A **12**
Martello Beach Cvn. Pk.
BN24: Pev B 6A **12**
Martello Ct. *BN24: Pev B* *6A* ***12***
(off Grenville Rd.)
Martello Rd. BN22: Eastb 1D **20**
Martello Rdbt. BN23: Eastb 3G **17**
Martin Ct. BN22: Eastb 3F **15**
Martinique Way BN23: Eastb 6G **17**
Martlets, The BN22: Will 2D **14**
BN27: Hails 2C **6**
Maryan Ct. BN27: Hails 1D **6**
Matlock Rd. BN20: Eastb 1G **23**
Maxfield Cl. BN20: Eastb 2D **18**
Mayfair Cl. BN26: Pole 1B **14**
Mayfair Ho. BN21: Eastb 3E **3** (5A **20**)
Mayfield Pl. BN22: Eastb 3A **20**
Mayo Ct. *BN23: Lang* *4D* ***16***
(off Pembury Rd.)
Maywood Av. BN22: Eastb 3F **15**
Meachants Ct. BN20: Will 3D **14**
Meachants La. BN20: Will 3C **14**
Meadhurst BN20: Eastb 5B **2**
Meadow Cl. BN27: Hails 6D **4**
Meadowlands Av. BN22: Eastb 3F **15**
Meadow Rd. BN27: Hails 3C **6**
Meadows Rd. BN22: Will 3D **14**
MEADS . . . .**6B 2 (1G 23)**
Meads Brow BN20: Eastb 1F **23**
Meads Ct. BN20: Eastb 5B **2** (6G **19**)
Meads Lodge BN21: Eastb 5D **2**
Meads Rd. BN20: Eastb 6A **2** (1G **23**)
Meads Rdbt. BN20: Eastb 1G **23**
Meads St. BN20: Eastb 1G **23**
Meadsway BN20: Eastb 1G **23**
Medina Dr. BN24: Sto C 6B **10**
Medway BN27: Hails 5C **4**
Medway La. BN24: Sto C 6A **10**
Melbourne Rd. BN22: Eastb 1G **3** (4B **20**)
Melrose Cl. BN27: Hails 1C **6**
Melvill La. BN20: Will 5D **14**
Memorial Rdbt. BN21: Eastb 3E **3**
Mendip Av. BN23: Lang 2C **16**
Meon Cl. BN24: Sto C 6A **10**
Merewood Ct. BN21: Eastb 3G **19**
Merlin Ct. BN27: Hails 2G **7**
Merlswood BN20: Eastb 5B **2** (6G **19**)
Merlynn BN21: Eastb 4F **3** (5A **20**)
Metropole Ct. BN22: Eastb 1H **3**
Mewett's Ct. BN20: Will 2D **14**
Mews, The BN22: Eastb 1D **20**
Michel Cl. BN20: E Dean 2C **22**
Michel Dene Cl. BN20: E Dean 2C **22**
Michel Dene Rd. BN20: E Dean, Fris 1C **22**
Michel Gro. BN21: Eastb 1A **2** (4G **19**)
Michel Gro. Ho. BN21: Eastb 1B **2** (4G **19**)
Michelham Cl. BN23: Lang 1A **16**
Middleham Way BN23: Lang 1C **16**
Middle Pde. BN20: Eastb 6E **3** (2G **23**)
BN21: Eastb 6F **3** (6A **20**)
Middlesex Ct. *BN22: Eastb* *3B* ***20***
(off Leslie St.)
Middleton Dr. BN23: Eastb 6E **17**
Midhurst Rd. BN22: Eastb 3H **15**
Midway Quay BN23: Eastb 5G **17**
Milchester Ho. *BN20: Eastb* *1G* ***23***
(off Buxton Rd.)
Milfoil Dr. BN23: Lang 1B **16**
Milland M. *BN27: Hails* *6D* ***4***
(off Milland Rd.)
Milland Rd. BN27: Hails 6D **4**
Millbrook Gdns. BN20: Eastb 1D **18**
Mill Cl. BN20: Fris 2A **22**
BN26: Pole 1B **14**
Mill Crest BN24: Sto C 6B **10**
Millers Ri. BN27: Hails 3C **6**
Millfield Ct. BN21: Eastb 1B **2**
Millfields Cl. BN26: Pole 4C **8**
Millfields Ct. BN26: Pole 4C **8**
Mill Gap Rd. BN21: Eastb 3H **19**
MILL HILL **4E 11**
Mill La. BN27: Hell 2C **4**
Millrace, The BN26: Pole 1B **14**
Mill Rd. BN21: Eastb 2F **19**
BN27: Hails 2E **7**
Millstream Gdns. BN26: Pole 1B **14**
Mill Vw. Cl. BN24: W'ham 5D **10**
Millward Rd. BN24: Pev B 6A **12**
Mill Way BN26: Pole 2A **14**
Milnthorpe Gdns. BN20: Eastb 1G **23**
Milnthorpe Rd. BN20: Eastb 1G **23**
Milton Cres. BN21: Eastb 3E **19**

Milton Grange *BN21: Eastb* ... *3H 19*
(off Arundel Rd.)
Milton Rd. BN21: Eastb ... 2E **19**
Milton St. BN24: Hank ... 5A **10**
Mimosa Cl. BN26: Pole ... 3C **8**
Mimram Rd. BN24: Sto C ... 6A **10**
Minster Cl. BN26: Pole ... 4C **8**
Mirasol BN20: Eastb ... 6C **2**
Moat Cft. Ct. BN21: Eastb ... 1A **2** (4G **19**)
Moat Cft. Rd. BN21: Eastb ... 1A **2** (4G **19**)
Moat Ho. BN21: Eastb ... 1A **2** (4G **19**)
Mole Cl. BN24: Sto C ... 6A **10**
Monarch Gdns. BN23: Lang ... 4F **17**
Monarch Ho. BN22: Eastb ... 1E **21**
Mona Rd. BN22: Eastb ... 3B **20**
Monceux Rd. BN21: Eastb ... 3E **19**
Monk Sherborne Ho.
BN20: Eastb ... 5C **2**
Monserrat Vs. BN23: Eastb ... 6G **17**
Montague Way BN24: W'ham ... 6F **11**
Montclare Ho. BN21: Eastb ... 1B **2**
Montfort Cl. BN24: W'ham ... 5F **11**
Montfort Rd. BN24: W'ham ... 5F **11**
Moore Pk. BN27: Hails ... 2F **7**
Moorings, The *BN20: Eastb* ... *1G 23*
(off St John's Rd.)
Moray Wlk. BN27: Hails ... 5C **4**
Mortain Pk. BN27: Hails ... 2F **7**
Mortain Rd. BN24: W'ham ... 5F **11**
Mortimer Gdns. BN26: Pole ... 1B **14**
Mortimer Rd. BN22: Eastb ... 1A **20**
Moss Ho. BN21: Eastb ... 3D **2** (5H **19**)
Motcombe La. BN21: Eastb ... 3F **19**
Motcombe Rd. BN21: Eastb ... 3F **19**
Motcombe Swimming Pool ... **3F 19**
Mount, The BN20: Eastb ... 6B **2** (6G **19**)
BN27: Hails ... 3E **7**
Mountain Ash Cl. BN27: Hails ... 1C **6**
Mountbatten Dr. BN23: Eastb ... 6E **17**
Mountfield Rd. BN22: Eastb ... 4H **15**
Mountfield Rdbt. BN22: Eastb ... 4H **15**
Mountney Bri. Bus. Pk.
BN24: W'ham ... 1F **17**
Mountney Dr. BN24: Pev B ... 3D **12**
Mountney Rd. BN21: Eastb ... 3E **19**
Mount Rd. BN20: Eastb ... 1H **23**
Mountview Ter. BN27: Hails ... 3E **7**
Mowbray Ct. BN21: Eastb ... 5F **3**
Moy Av. BN22: Eastb ... 2A **20**
Mulberry Cl. BN22: Eastb ... 2G **15**
Mulberry Ct. *BN26: Pole* ... *5C 8*
(off Walnut Wlk.)
MULBROOKS ... **6D 6**
Musgrave Mus. ... **3G 3 (5B 20)**
Myrtle Rd. BN22: Eastb ... 1D **20**

N

Naomi Cl. BN20: Eastb ... 5B **2** (6G **19**)
Nelson Dr. BN23: Eastb ... 1E **21**
Netherfield Av. BN23: Lang ... 3F **17**
Nevill Av. BN22: Eastb ... 4G **15**
Neville Rd. BN22: Eastb ... 3B **20**
New Barn Cl. BN27: Hails ... 3E **7**
New Bridge Rd. BN27: Herst, Rick ... 1C **10**
New Coll. Cl. BN23: Lang ... 1C **16**
New Derby Ho. BN23: Eastb ... 6D **16**
Newick Rd. BN20: Eastb ... 1E **19**
New Langney Ct. BN23: Lang ... 4E **17**
New North St. BN27: Hails ... 4A **4**
New Pl. BN21: Eastb ... 4F **19**
New Rd. BN22: Eastb ... 1G **3** (3B **20**)
BN26: Pole ... 5D **8**
BN27: Hell ... 3D **4**
Newton Pk. BN27: Hails ... 2F **7**
New Upperton Rd.
BN21: Eastb ... 3G **19**
New Villas *BN26: Pole* ... *5D 8*
(off Western Av.)
NHS WALK-IN CENTRE
Eastbourne Station ... **2D 2**
Nicholson Ct. BN23: Lang ... 4E **17**
Nightingale Cl. BN23: Lang ... 3C **16**
BN26: Pole ... 4B **8**
Nodes La. BN27: Mag D ... 3H **5**
Norfolk Ct. *BN22: Eastb* ... *3C 20*
(off Redoubt Rd.)
Norman Rd. BN24: Pev B ... 5B **12**
NORMAN'S BAY ... **1H 13**
Norman's Bay Camping & Caravanning Pk.
BN24: Nor B ... 2F **13**
Normans Bay Caravan Pk.
BN24: Nor B ... 1G **13**
Norman's Bay Station (Rail) ... **1G 13**
North Av. BN20: Eastb ... 2D **18**
Northbourne Rd. BN22: Eastb ... 6B **16**
North Cl. BN26: Pole ... 4D **8**
North Cres. Ind. Est. BN27: Hails ... 2C **6**
Northern Av. BN26: Pole ... 4D **8**
Northfield BN26: Pole ... 6B **8**
Nth. Heath Cl. BN27: Hails ... 5E **5**
Northiam Rd. BN20: Eastb ... 3E **19**
BN21: Eastb ... 3E **19**
North Rd. BN24: Pev B ... 5B **12**
North St. BN21: Eastb ... 2G **3** (5B **20**)
BN27: Hails ... 1D **6**
BN27: Hell ... 2B **4**
Northumberland Ct. BN22: Eastb ... 3A **16**
Norway Rd. BN22: Eastb ... 1D **20**
Nursery Cl. BN26: Pole ... 5D **8**
BN27: Hails ... 1E **7**
Nursery Path BN27: Hails ... 3D **6**
Nutbourne Cl. *BN23: Lang* ... *3E 17*
(off Spring Lodge Cl.)
Nuthatch Rd. BN23: Lang ... 3C **16**
Nutley Mill Rd. BN24: Sto C ... 6B **10**

O

Oaklands BN21: Eastb ... 3A **20**
BN24: W'ham ... 5D **10**
Oaklands Cl. BN26: Pole ... 5D **8**
Oaklands Way BN27: Hails ... 3C **6**
Oakleaf Ct. BN26: Pole ... 4C **8**
Oakleaf Dr. BN26: Pole ... 4C **8**
Oakley Down BN20: Eastb ... 6B **2** (6G **19**)
Oak Tree Cl. BN23: Lang ... 1C **16**
Oak Tree La. BN23: Lang ... 1C **16**
Oaktree Way BN27: Hails ... 5E **5**
Oakwood Ho. BN21: Eastb ... 6D **2**
Observatory Vw. BN27: Hails ... 2F **7**
Ocho Rios M. BN23: Eastb ... 5F **17**
Ocklynge Av. BN21: Eastb ... 3F **19**
Ocklynge Rd. BN21: Eastb ... 1A **2** (3F **19**)
Offham Cl. BN23: Lang ... 1H **15**
Okehurst Rd. BN21: Eastb ... 4E **19**
Old Barn Cl. BN20: Will ... 4D **14**
Old Camp Rd. BN20: Eastb ... 5E **19**
Old Dr. BN26: Pole ... 5B **8**
Old Drove BN23: Lang ... 2C **16**
Oldfield Av. BN20: Will ... 1C **14**
Oldfield Cres. BN27: Hails ... 6D **4**
Oldfield Rd. BN20: Will ... 1C **14**
Old Mansion Cl. BN20: Will ... 5C **14**
Old Martello Rd. BN24: Pev B ... 3H **17**
Old Mill Cl. BN27: Hails ... 4C **4**
Old Mill La. BN26: Pole ... 2A **14**
Old Motcombe M. BN21: Eastb ... 3F **19**
Old Orchard Pl. BN27: Hails ... 2D **6**
Old Orchard Rd. BN21: Eastb ... 3C **2** (5H **19**)
Old Rd. BN27: Herst, Mag D ... 4H **5**
Old School, The *BN22: Eastb* ... *2C 20*
(off Whitley Rd.)
Old School Cl. BN26: Pole ... 4C **8**
Old Swan La. BN27: Hails ... 4F **7**
OLD TOWN ... **1A 2 (4F 19)**
Old Willingdon Rd. BN20: Fris ... 2A **22**
Old Wish Rd. BN21: Eastb ... 5D **2** (6H **19**)
Ollier Ct. BN20: Eastb ... 5D **2** (6H **19**)
Orchard, The *BN20: Will* ... *4D 14*
(off Church St.)
Orchard Pde. BN20: Will ... 2C **14**
Orchid Cl. BN23: Lang ... 2B **16**
Orion Cl. BN27: Hails ... 2F **7**
Orkney Ct. BN20: Eastb ... 1D **18**
Orvis Ct. BN23: Eastb ... 5G **17**
Orwell Cl. BN24: Sto C ... 6B **10**
Osborne Rd. BN20: Eastb ... 3D **18**
Otham Ct. La. BN26: Pole ... 3C **8**
Otham Pk. BN27: Hails ... 2F **7**
Otham Rd. BN22: Eastb ... 3A **16**
Otteham Cl. BN26: Pole ... 5D **8**
Oulton Cl. BN23: Lang ... 2B **16**
Outlook, The BN20: Fris ... 2A **22**
Oxendean Gdns. BN22: Will ... 1D **14**
Oxford Rd. BN22: Eastb ... 3B **20**

P

Pacific Dr. BN23: Eastb ... 4G **17**
Pacific Hgts. Nth. BN23: Eastb ... 4G **17**
Pacific Hgts. Sth. BN23: Eastb ... 4G **17**
Paddock, The BN22: Eastb ... 3H **15**
Paddock Gdns. BN26: Pole ... 1B **14**
Paddocks, The BN27: Hails ... 5C **4**
Pagham Cl. BN23: Lang ... 1B **16**
Palesgate Way BN20: Eastb ... 2D **18**
Palgrave Ho. BN22: Eastb ... 1H **3**
Palliser Cl. BN23: Eastb ... 1E **21**
Palma Cl. BN26: Pole ... 4C **8**
Palmers Row BN27: Hails ... 2D **6**
Palmyra Pl. BN23: Eastb ... 5G **17**
Palomar Ct. BN23: Eastb ... 5G **17**
Parade, The BN24: Pev B ... 4B **12**
(Seaville Dr.)
BN24: Pev B ... 3D **12**
(Westham Dr.)
Paradise Cl. BN20: Eastb ... 5F **19**
Paradise Dr.
BN20: Eastb ... 3A **2** & 6A **2** (6E **19**)
Paragon, The BN20: Will ... 2B **14**
Park Av. BN21: Eastb ... 6E **15**
BN22: Eastb ... 6F **15**
Park Cl. BN20: Eastb ... 2A **2** (4F **19**)
BN27: Hails ... 3D **6**
Park Cft. BN26: Pole ... 1C **14**
Parker Cl. BN21: Eastb ... 2G **19**
Parker Ho. *BN22: Eastb* ... *3C 20*
(off Redoubt Rd.)
Parkfield Av. BN22: Eastb ... 4F **15**
Park Gate BN27: Hails ... 4F **5**
Park Gates BN21: Eastb ... 4F **3** (5A **20**)
Parkholme BN20: Eastb ... 6B **2**
Park Ho. BN21: Eastb ... 4F **3**
(Burlington Pl.)
BN21: Eastb ... 4E **3** (5A **20**)
(Spencer Rd.)
Park La. BN21: Will ... 5E **15**
Park Lodge BN21: Eastb ... 4F **3**
(Devonshire Pl.)
BN21: Eastb ... 4E **3**
(Wish Rd.)
Park Rd. BN27: Hell ... 3D **4**
Park Vw. BN23: Eastb ... 5C **16**
Parkway BN20: Will ... 5C **14**
Parry Cl. BN23: Lang ... 2E **17**
Parsonage Rd. BN21: Eastb ... 3F **19**
Pashley Ct. BN20: Eastb ... 5E **19**
Pashley Rd. BN20: Eastb ... 5D **18**
Patcham Mill Rd. BN24: Sto C ... 6B **10**
Paul Cl. BN27: Hails ... 4C **4**
Pauling Ho. BN21: Eastb ... 4E **3**
Peakdean Cl. BN20: Fris ... 1B **22**
Peakdean La. BN20: Fris ... 1C **22**
Pearl Ct. BN21: Eastb ... 3F
Pebble Rd. BN24: Pev B ... 4C **12**
Peel Ho. Farm Caravan Pk.
BN26: Pole ... 6D
Peelings La. BN24: Sto C, W'ham ... 6B **1**
Pelham Cl. BN24: W'ham ... 6F **1**
Pelham Cres. BN27: Hails ... 3E
Pembroke Cl. BN27: Hails ... 4E
Pembroke Ho. BN21: Eastb ... 1C
Pembury Rd. BN23: Lang ... 4D **1**
Penhale Rd. BN22: Eastb ... 2D **2**
Penhurst Cl. BN22: Eastb ... 4A **1**

Pennine Way BN23: Lang 2C 16
Penrith Way BN23: Lang 1C 16
Pensford Dr. BN23: Lang 2D 16
Penshurst Ho. *BN22: Eastb 1D 20*
(off Groombridge Av.)
Pentland Cl. BN23: Lang 2E 17
Peppercombe Rd. BN20: Eastb 3D 18
Pepys Wlk. *BN23: Lang 3E 17*
(off The Rising)
Percival Cres. BN22: Eastb 2H 15
Percival Rd. BN22: Eastb 2H 15
Perth Ct. BN21: Eastb 3A 20
Petworth Pl. BN22: Eastb 3G 15
PEVENSEY 5H 11
Pevensey & Westham Station (Rail) 6F 11
PEVENSEY BAY 4B 12
Pevensey Bay Rd. BN23: Eastb 5E 17
Pevensey Bay Sailing Club 6A 12
Pevensey Bay Station (Rail) 3A 12
Pevensey By-Pass
BN24: Hank, Pev, Sto C, W'ham 5H 9
Pevensey Castle 5G 11
Pevensey Ct. *BN24: Pev B 4B 12*
(off Eastbourne Rd.)
Pevensey Courthouse Mus. 5H 11
Pevensey Levels National Nature Reserve
. . . . .1B 12
Pevensey Pk. Rd. BN24: W'ham 5F 11
Pevensey Rd. BN21: Eastb 2F 3 (4A 20)
BN22: Eastb 2G 3 (4A 20)
BN26: Pole 5D 8
Pevensey Rdbt. BN24: Pev 2A 12
Peyton Cl. BN23: Eastb 6F 17
Phoenix Cl. BN27: Hails 2F 7
Phoenix Ct. BN22: Eastb 1H 3
Phoenix Dr. BN23: Eastb 5G 17
Piazza, The BN23: Eastb 5F 17
Pierpoint M. *BN23: Eastb 4G 17*
(off Belvedere)
Piltdown Way BN23: Lang 1A 16
Pine Way BN27: Hails 2C 6
Pinewood Cl. BN22: Eastb 3F 15
Pitcairn Av. BN23: Eastb 3H 17
Pitreavie Dr. BN27: Hails 1C 6
Plover Cl. BN23: Lang 3C 16
Plumpton Cl. BN23: Lang 1A 16
Plymouth Cl. BN23: Eastb 5F 17
Pocock's Rd. BN21: Eastb 2F 19
POLEGATE .5C 8
Polegate By-Pass BN26: Hank, Pole 2B 8
Polegate Rd. BN27: Hails 4C 6
Polegate Station (Rail) 5C 8
Polegate Towermill 6C 8
Polegate Towermill Milling Mus. *6C 8*
Polly Arch Caravan Site BN26: Pole 5E 9
Poplar Wlk. BN22: Eastb 2F 15
Porters Way BN26: Pole 5C 8
Portland Cl. BN27: Hails 6C 4
Portlands, The BN23: Eastb 6F 17
Port Rd. BN22: Eastb 4A 16
Portsdown Way BN20: Will 3D 14
Potts Marsh Ind. Est. BN24: W'ham 6F 11
Pound Cl. BN23: Eastb 1F 21
Prideaux Ct. BN21: Eastb 2H 19
Prideaux Rd. BN21: Eastb 2G 19
Pride Vw. BN24: Sto C 6B 10
Primrose Cl. BN23: Lang 2B 16
Princes Pk. 2D 20
Princes Rd. BN23: Eastb 1E 21
Prince William Pde. BN23: Eastb 1E 21
Priory Cl. BN24: Pev B 4B 12
Priory Ct. BN20: Eastb 5C 2
Priory Hgts. BN20: Eastb 2C 18
Priory La. BN23: Lang 2E 17
Priory Lane Stadium 2F 17
Priory Orchard BN23: Lang 4E 17
Priory Rd. BN23: Lang 2E 17
Priory Rdbt. BN23: Lang 2E 17
Promenade BN21: Eastb 3H 3 (5B 20)
BN22: Eastb 1H 3 (4C 20)
BN23: Eastb 1F 21
Promenade, The BN24: Pev B 5B 12
Prospect Gdns. BN21: Eastb 3F 19
Pulborough Av. BN22: Eastb 4G 15
Purbeck Cl. BN23: Lang 1C 16

Q

Quadrant, The BN21: Eastb 3G 19
Quantock Cl. BN23: Lang 2D 16
Quebec Cl. BN23: Eastb 6F 17
Queen Alexandra's Cott. Homes
BN23: Eastb 6D 16
(off Seaside)
Queens Cliff *BN21: Eastb 3H 19*
(off Carew Rd.)
Queens Ct. BN23: Eastb 6D 16
Queen's Cres. BN23: Eastb 6D 16
Queen's Gdns. BN21: Eastb 2H 3 (4B 20)
Queens Ride BN20: Will 2B 14
Queen's Rd. BN23: Eastb 6D 16
Quinnell Dr. BN27: Hails 5D 4
Quintin Cl. BN27: Hails 4C 6
Quintins, The BN27: Hails 1E 7

R

Raglan Ct. BN24: Pev B 6A 12
Rainey Ct. BN21: Eastb 1G 3 (4B 20)
Raleigh Cl. BN23: Eastb 1E 21
Ramsay Way BN23: Eastb 6E 17
Ranelagh Ct. BN23: Eastb 1E 21
Rangemore Dr. BN21: Eastb 6F 15
Ranworth Cl. BN23: Lang 1B 16
Rapala Ct. BN23: Eastb 5G 17
Rapson's Rd. BN20: Will 2B 14
Rattle Rd.
BN24: Sto C, W'ham 6B 10
Ratton Dr. BN20: Will 6D 14
Ratton Gdns. BN20: Will 6D 14
Ratton Rd. BN21: Eastb 3G 19
RATTON VILLAGE 6D 14
Ravens Ct. *BN20: Eastb 1H 23*
(off St John's Rd.)
Ravens Cft. BN20: Eastb 1H 23
Rectory Cl. BN20: Eastb 4F 19
Red Dyke Cotts. BN24: Sto C 5H 9
Redford Cl. BN23: Lang 4E 17
Redman King Ho.
BN20: Eastb 4C 2 (5H 19)
Redoubt Fortress & Military Mus. 3C 20
Redoubt Rd. BN22: Eastb 3C 20
Reedham Rd. BN23: Lang 1B 16
Regency Ct. BN20: Eastb 1H 23
Regency M. BN20: Eastb 6E 3 (6A 20)
Regents Pl. BN21: Eastb 5F 15
Regnum Cl. BN22: Eastb 1G 15
Reid Cres. BN27: Hell 2F 5
Renascent Ho. BN21: Eastb 2G 3
Renfrew Ct. *BN22: Eastb 1D 20*
(off Allfrey Rd.)
Residence, The BN22: Eastb 1H 3
Reynolds Rd. BN23: Lang 4D 16
Reynoldstown La. BN26: Pole 5B 8
Richmond Pl. BN21: Eastb 1C 2 (3H 19)
Richmond Rd. BN24: Pev B 4B 12
Rickard Gdns. BN27: Hell 2F 5
RICKNEY 1C 10
Rickney La.
BN27: Down, Pev, Rick . . . . .5G 7 & 1A 10
Rickney Rd. BN24: Hank 2B 10
BN27: Hank, Pev, Rick 2B 10
Ridge, The BN20: Eastb 1H 23
Ridgelands Cl. BN20: Eastb 4E 19
Ridgeway, The BN20: Fris 2A 22
Ringmer Way BN23: Lang 1A 16
Ringwood Cl. BN22: Eastb 2B 20
Ringwood Ct. BN22: Eastb 2C 20
Ringwood Rd. BN22: Eastb 2A 20
Ripley Chase BN21: Eastb 1B 2 (4G 19)
Ripsley Cl. BN23: Lang 3E 17
Rise Pk. Gdns. BN23: Lang 3D 16
Rising, The BN23: Lang 3D 16
Riverbourne Ho. BN22: Eastb . . .1H 3 (3B 20)
Robert Ho. *BN21: Eastb 3H 19*
(off Carew Rd.)
Robin Cl. BN23: Lang 3C 16
Robin Post La. BN26: Hails 1A 8
BN27: Hails .5A 6
Robinson Ct. BN22: Eastb 1C 20
Roborough Cl. BN21: Eastb 3A 20
Roborough Ct. BN21: Eastb 3A 20
Rochester Cl. BN20: Eastb 1E 23
Rockall Av. BN23: Eastb 5F 17
Rockall Dr. BN27: Hails 5C 4
Rockhurst Dr. BN20: Eastb 1D 18
Rocky's Adventure Land *2E 21*
(part of Fort Fun)
Rodmill Dr. BN21: Eastb 2F 19
Rodmill Rd. BN21: Eastb 2F 19
Rodmill Rdbt. BN21: Eastb 1G 19
Rodney Cl. BN23: Eastb 6E 17
Roffrey Av. BN22: Eastb 4F 15
Roman Cft. BN21: Eastb 3G 19
Romans Way BN24: W'ham 5E 11
Romney Rd. BN26: Pole 4D 8
Romney St. BN22: Eastb 2C 20
Rookery, The BN23: Lang 1C 16
Rookery Farm Caravan Site
BN23: Lang 1C 16
Ropemaker Pk. BN27: Hails 2D 6
Rope Wlk. BN27: Hails 1D 6
Rosebery Av. BN22: Eastb 4G 15
Rosedale Pl. BN22: Eastb 2F 15
Roseland Ct. *BN22: Eastb 2C 20*
(off Seaside)
ROSELANDS 2C 20
Roselands Av. BN22: Eastb 1C 20
Roselands Cl. BN22: Eastb 2C 20
Rosemullion BN20: Eastb 6B 2
Rosetti Rd. BN24: Pev B 5A 12
Roseveare Rd. BN22: Eastb 1B 20
Rossington Cl. BN21: Eastb 2F 19
Rother Av. BN24: Sto C 6H 9
Rotherfield Av. BN23: Lang 1A 16
Rotunda Rd. BN23: Eastb 5D 16
Rowan Av. BN22: Eastb 2F 15
Rowan Ct. *BN26: Pole 5C 8*
(off Walnut Wlk.)
Rowsley Rd. BN20: Eastb 2F 23
Roxburgh Ct. BN23: Lang 2D 16
Royal Eastbourne Golf Course
. . . . .3A 2 (5G 19)
Royal Hippodrome Theatre 2H 3 (4B 20)
Royal Pde. BN22: Eastb 1H 3 (4C 20)
Royal Sovereign Vw. BN23: Eastb 1F 21
Royal Sussex Cres. BN20: Eastb 2D 18
Royston Cl. BN20: Fris 2A 22
Rubislaw Ct. BN21: Eastb 3H 19
Rush Ct. BN22: Eastb 1G 3 (4B 20)
Rushlake Cres. BN21: Eastb 1F 19
Ruskin Rd. BN20: Will 4D 14
Rusper Ho. BN21: Eastb 1B 2
Rusper Rd. BN20: Eastb 1D 18
Russet Cl. BN26: Pole 5E 9
Rustington Ct. BN20: Eastb 6D 2 (1H 23)
Rutland Cl. BN21: Eastb 1F 19
Rutland Ct. BN23: Lang 4E 17
Ruxley Ct. BN23: Lang 3D 16
Rydal Way BN23: Lang 1B 16
Rye Cl. BN26: Pole 4E 9
Ryefield Cl. BN21: Will 6E 15
Rye St. BN22: Eastb 1D 20
Rylstone Rd. BN22: Eastb 3C 20

S

Sackville Rd. BN22: Eastb 3H 15
BN27: Hails .3E 7
Saddlers M. BN21: Eastb 2H 3
Saffrons Ct. BN20: Eastb 4B 2 (5G 19)
Saffrons Ga. BN20: Eastb 4C 2 (5H 19)
Saffrons Mead BN20: Eastb 4C 2 (5H 19)
Saffrons Pk. BN20: Eastb 5A 2 (6G 19)
Saffrons Rd. BN21: Eastb 2B 2 (4G 19)
St Aidans Ct. BN22: Eastb 2C 20

St Andrews Cl. BN27: Hails .6C **4**
St Annes Rd. BN20: Will .2D **14**
BN21: Eastb .1C **2** (3G **19**)
St Anthony's Av. BN23: Eastb .5E **17**
ST ANTHONY'S HILL .6D **16**
St Aubyn's Rd. BN22: Eastb .1H **3** (4B **20**)
St Boswells Cl. BN27: Hails .1C **6**
St Brelades BN21: Eastb .4G **3**
St Clements Ct. BN21: Eastb .1F **19**
St Davids Cl. BN22: Eastb .1F **15**
St Denys BN21: Eastb .3G **19**
St Emmanuel Ho. *BN20: Eastb .2G* ***23***
(off Darley Rd.)
St Gabriel Ho. BN20: Eastb .2G **23**
St Georges BN21: Eastb .3E **19**
St George's Rd. BN22: Eastb .3B **20**
St Gregory Cl. BN20: Eastb .6A **2** (1G **23**)
St Helena Ct. BN21: Eastb .3G **19**
St Ives Ct. BN21: Eastb .3H **19**
St James BN24: Nor B .1H **13**
St James Rd. BN22: Eastb .3C **20**
St John's Ct. BN26: Pole .5C **8**
St John's Dr. BN24: W'ham .5E **11**
St Johns Ho. BN20: Eastb .6C **2**
St John's Rd. BN20: Eastb .6D **2** (1G **23**)
BN26: Pole .5C **8**
St Kilda Mans. BN21: Eastb .1C **2**
St Kitts Dr. BN23: Eastb .6G **17**
St Lawrence M. BN23: Eastb .4G **17**
St Lawrence Pl. BN23: Eastb .4G **17**
St Lawrence Way BN23: Eastb .4G **17**
St Leonard's Pl. BN20: Eastb .4E **19**
St Leonard's Rd. BN21: Eastb .1D **2** (4H **19**)
St Leonards Ter. BN26: Pole .4B **8**
St Lucia Wlk. BN23: Eastb .5F **17**
St Martins Rd. BN22: Eastb .1F **15**
St Mary's BN26: Pole .5E **9**
St Mary's Av. BN27: Hails .2E **7**
St Mary's Cl. BN22: Will .3D **14**
St Mary's Cotts. BN20: Eastb .1A **2** (4F **19**)
St Marys Ct. BN21: Eastb .1A **2** (4F **19**)
St Mary's Rd. BN21: Eastb .3F **19**
St Marys Wlk. *BN27: Hails .2E* ***7***
(off High St.)
St Mellion Cl. BN27: Hails .1B **6**
St Michaels Cl. BN24: Sto C .5A **10**
St Nicholas Cl. BN24: Pev .5H **11**
St Paul's Cl. BN22: Eastb .2F **15**
St Philips Av. BN22: Eastb .2B **20**
St Philips Pl. BN22: Eastb .2B **20**
St Ritas BN20: Eastb .6A **2** (6F **19**)
St Saviour Ho. BN20: Eastb .2G **23**
St Vincents Pl. BN20: Eastb .6A **2** (6G **19**)
St Wilfrid's Grn. BN27: Hails .1E **7**
St Wilfrid's Hospice
Mill Gap Rd. .3H **19**
Broadwater Way (Opens late 2013)
.5G **15**
Salehurst Rd. BN21: Eastb .4E **19**
Salisbury Cl. BN22: Will .3E **15**
Salisbury Rd. BN20: Eastb .1E **23**
Saltmarsh La. BN27: Down, Hails .5E **7**
Salvador Cl. BN23: Eastb .6F **17**
Samoa Way BN23: Eastb .3H **17**
Sancroft Rd. BN20: Eastb .4D **18**
Sanctuary, The BN20: Eastb .3D **18**
Sandbanks Cl. BN27: Hails .4C **6**
Sandbanks Gdns. BN27: Hails .4D **6**
Sandbanks Gro. BN27: Hails .3D **6**
Sandbanks Way BN27: Hails .3C **6**
Sandford M. *BN23: Lang .2D* ***16***
(off Pensford Dr.)
Sandhurst M. BN23: Lang .4E **17**
San Diego Way BN23: Eastb .4H **17**
Sandown Cl. BN23: Lang .1A **16**
Sandpiper Wlk. BN23: Lang .3C **16**
Sandwich St. BN22: Eastb .1C **20**
San Juan Ct. BN23: Eastb .6G **17**
Sanshaw Ct. BN21: Eastb .1A **2** (4G **19**)
Santa Cruz Dr. BN23: Eastb .6F **17**
Santos Wharf BN23: Eastb .5F **17**
Saxby Cl. BN23: Lang .4E **17**
Saxon Cl. BN27: Hails .4F **5**
Saxon Ct. BN21: Eastb .2H **3**
Saxon Ground BN21: Eastb .3G **19**
Saxon Pl. BN21: Eastb .1E **19**
SAYERLAND .3C **8**
Sayerland La. BN26: Pole .3C **8**
Sayerland Rd. BN26: Pole .4B **8**
Scanlan Cl. BN20: Will .2C **14**
Schofield Way BN23: Eastb .6F **17**
School La. BN26: Pole .4C **8**
Scotney Ho. BN22: Eastb .1E **21**
Seabeach La. BN22: Eastb .2C **20**
Seaford Rd. BN20: Fris .2A **22**
BN22: Eastb .2C **20**
Seaforth Ct. BN20: Eastb .4E **19**
Sea Rd. BN24: Pev B .4B **12**
Seaside BN21: Eastb .2H **3** (4B **20**)
BN22: Eastb .2H **3** (4B **20**)
BN23: Eastb .6D **16**
Seaside Rd. BN21: Eastb .3G **3** (5B **20**)
Seaside Rdbt. BN22: Eastb .6D **16**
Seattle Dr. BN23: Eastb .4G **17**
Seaville Dr. BN23: Eastb .5D **16**
BN24: Pev B .4B **12**
Selby Rd. BN21: Eastb .2F **19**
Selmeston Ho. BN21: Eastb .3F **19**
Selmeston Rd. BN21: Eastb .6E **15**
Selsfield Cl. BN21: Eastb .1F **19**
Selwyn Dr. BN21: Eastb .3G **19**
Selwyn Ho. BN21: Eastb .3G **19**
Selwyn Pk. Ct. BN21: Eastb .3G **19**
Selwyn Rd. BN21: Eastb .1B **2** (3G **19**)
Sevenoaks Rd. BN23: Lang .3B **16**
Seven Sisters Rd. BN22: Eastb, Will .2D **14**
Seven Sisters Sheep Cen. .4B **22**
Shackleton Cl. BN21: Eastb .2G **3** (4B **20**)
Shakespeare Wlk. BN23: Lang .3E **17**
Shalfleet Cl. BN23: Lang .2B **16**
Shanklin Cl. BN23: Lang .1B **16**
Shannon Way BN23: Eastb .5F **17**
Sheen Rd. BN22: Eastb .3B **20**
Sheffield Pk. Way BN23: Lang .1A **16**
Shelley Wlk. BN23: Lang .3E **17**
Shepham La. BN26: Pole .4E **9**
Shepherds Cl. BN22: Eastb .2H **15**
Sheppey Wlk. BN27: Hails .4C **4**
Sheraton Cl. BN21: Eastb .4D **2** (5H **19**)
Sherbourne Ct. *BN21: Eastb .3F* ***19***
(off Upperton Rd.)
Sherwood Ct. BN21: Eastb .3F **3**
Sherwood Grn. BN27: Hails .3D **6**
Shetland Cl. BN27: Hails .4C **4**
Shinewater Ct. BN23: Lang .2B **16**
Shinewater La. BN23: Lang .2B **16**
(not continuous)
Shinewater Rdbt. BN23: Eastb .4B **16**
Shipley Mill Cl. BN24: Sto C .6B **10**
Short Brow Cl. BN22: Will .2D **14**
Shortdean Pl. BN21: Eastb .3F **19**
Shortlands Cl. BN22: Will .4E **15**
Shropshire Ct. BN20: Eastb .6D **14**
Sidcup Cl. BN23: Lang .3D **16**
Sidings, The BN22: Eastb .1B **20**
BN27: Hails .3E **7**
Sidley Rd. BN22: Eastb .3C **20**
Silverdale Ct. BN20: Eastb .6D **2** (6H **19**)
BN27: Hails .1D **6**
Silverdale Rd. BN20: Eastb .6B **2** (6G **19**)
Silver Strand E. BN23: Eastb .4G **17**
Silver Strand W. BN23: Eastb .4G **17**
Singleton Mill Rd. BN24: Sto C .6C **10**
Slindon Cres. BN23: Lang .4E **17**
(not continuous)
Sluice Rd. BN24: Pev .2A **12**
Snapson's Drove BN27: Hails, Rick .3H **7**
Snowdon Cl. BN23: Lang .2D **16**
Solent Cres. BN27: Hails .4B **4**
Solly Ct. BN21: Eastb .1G **3** (4B **20**)
Solomons Cl. BN23: Eastb .3H **17**
Solway BN27: Hails .5C **4**
Somerset Ct. BN23: Lang .4E **17**
Somerville Cl. BN23: Eastb .6E **17**
Sorrel Cl. BN23: Lang .2C **16**
Sorrel Dr. BN23: Lang .1B **16**
Southampton Cl. BN23: Eastb .5F **17**
South Av. BN20: Eastb .2D **18**
Southbourne Bus. Pk. BN22: Eastb .2A **20**
Southbourne Rd. BN22: Eastb .1C **20**
South Cliff BN20: Eastb .6D **2** (1H **23**)
Sth. Cliff Av. BN20: Eastb .6D **2** (6H **19**)
Sth. Cliff Twr. BN20: Eastb .1H **23**
South Cl. BN24: Pev B .3D **12**
BN27: Hails .3D **6**
South Coast Falconry & Conservation Cen.
.2A **6**
Southdown Av. BN20: Will .2C **14**
Southdown Cotts. BN20: Will .2C **14**
Southdown Ct. *BN27: Hails .2E* ***7***
(off Bell Banks Rd.)
Southdown Ho. BN20: Eastb .6D **2** (6H **19**)
Southdown Rd. BN20: Eastb .6D **14**
South Downs National Pk. .5B **14** & 5E **23**
South Elms BN20: Eastb .6B **2**
Southerden Cl. BN27: Hails .2E **7**
Southern Av. BN26: Pole .5D **8**
Southern Rd. BN22: Eastb .3H **15**
Southfield BN26: Pole .6B **8**
Southfields Ct. BN21: Eastb .2C **2**
Southfields Rd. BN21: Eastb .1B **2** (4G **19**)
South Lynn Dr. BN21: Eastb .3H **19**
South Rd. BN27: Hails .3C **6**
South St. BN21: Eastb .3D **2** (5H **19**)
(not continuous)
South Vw. BN21: Eastb .3G **19**
Sovereign Cen. .1E **21**
Sovereign Ct. BN22: Eastb .2C **20**
SOVEREIGN HARBOUR .4G **17**
Sovereign Harbour Marina .5G **17**
Sovereign Harbour Retail Pk.
BN23: Eastb .4F **17**
Sovereign Harbour Yacht Club .4G **17**
Sovereign Ho. BN21: Eastb .3G **3**
Sovereign Rdbt. BN22: Eastb .1E **21**
Spencer Ct. BN21: Eastb .4E **3**
Spencer Ho. BN21: Eastb .4E **3**
Spencer Rd. BN21: Eastb .4E **3** (5A **20**)
Spring Cl. BN20: Will .4D **14**
Springfield Cl. BN24: W'ham .5F **11**
Springfield Rd. BN22: Eastb .3B **20**
Spring Lodge Cl. BN23: Lang .3E **17**
Spruce Cl. BN22: Eastb .3F **15**
Spur Rd. BN26: Pole .6D **8**
Spurway Pk. BN26: Pole .6D **8**
Squab La. BN27: Mag D .2H **5**
Square, The BN24: Pev B .3D **12**
BN27: Hails .2C **6**
Stables La. BN21: Eastb .2E **3**
Stafford Ct. *BN23: Lang .4E* ***17***
(off Etchingham Rd.)
Stafford Ho. BN21: Eastb .2D **2**
Standen Ho. *BN22: Eastb .1E* ***21***
(off Groombridge Av.)
Stanhope Ct. BN20: Eastb .6C **2**
Stanley Rd. BN22: Eastb .3B **20**
Stanmer Dr. BN22: Will .4F **15**
Stanmer Ho. BN21: Eastb .4D **2** (5H **19**)
Stansted Rd. BN22: Eastb .3A **20**
Stanton Prior BN20: Eastb .1F **23**
Star Rd. BN21: Eastb .1A **2** (4G **19**)
Station App. BN22: Eastb .4H **15**
Station Pde. BN21: Eastb .2D **2**
Station Rd. BN26: Pole .4C **8**
BN27: Hails .2D **6**
BN27: Hell .2C **4**
Station Rd. Ind. Est. BN27: Hails .3E **7**
Station Rdbt. BN21: Eastb .2D **2** (4H **19**)
Station St. BN21: Eastb .2D **2** (4A **20**)
Staveley Ct. *BN20: Eastb .1G* ***2***
(off Staveley Rd.)
Staveley Mead *BN20: Eastb .1G* ***2***
(off Buxton Rd.)
Staveley Rd. BN20: Eastb .1G **2**
Steeple Grange BN21: Eastb .3G **1**
Stevenson Cl. BN23: Lang .2E **1**
Stiles, The BN27: Hails .2E
Stirling Ct. BN23: Lang .4E **1**
STONE CROSS .6A **1**

Stone Cross Towermill .6B 10
Stonegate Cl. BN23: Lang .1A 16
Stoney Down *BN20: Eastb* .1G 23
(off Milnthorpe Rd.)
Stoney La. BN27: Hails .2E 7
Stour Cl. BN24: Sto C .6H 9
Stratford Ho. BN21: Eastb .1G 3
Stringwalk, The BN27: Hails .2E 7
Stroma Gdns. BN27: Hails .5B 4
Stuart Av. BN21: Eastb .1E 19
Stud Farm Stables, The BN26: Pole .5A 8
Sturdee Cl. BN23: Eastb .6F 17
Sturton Pl. BN27: Hails .2D 6
Suffolk Ct. BN22: Eastb .3C 20
Sumach Cl. BN22: Eastb .3G 15
Summer Ct. BN20: Eastb .2F 23
BN27: Hails .1D 6
Summerdown Cl. BN20: Eastb .4F 19
Summerdown La. BN20: E Dean .2C 22
Summerdown Rd. BN20: Eastb .4E 19
Summerfields Av. BN27: Hails .1C 6
Summerheath Rd. BN27: Hails .1D 6
SUMMER HILL .6C 6
Summer Hill La. BN26: Pole .6B 6
Summerlands Rd. BN22: Will .3D 14
Sunningdale Cl. BN27: Hails .6C 4
Sunnymead BN20: Eastb .6A 2 (1G 23)
Sun Patch BN27: Hails .2E 7
Sunset Cl. BN24: Pev B .3C 12
Sunstar La. BN26: Pole .5A 8
Susan's Rd. BN21: Eastb .1F 3 (4A 20)
Sussex Av. BN27: Hails .1D 6
Sussex Cl. BN27: Hails .1D 6
Sussex Ct. BN22: Eastb .2B 20
Sussex Gdns. BN20: E Dean .2C 22
Sussex Ho. BN21: Eastb .3F 3
Sussex Mans. *BN21: Eastb* .3E 3
(off Cornfield Ter.)
Sutton Ho. BN20: Eastb .6B 2
Sutton Rd. BN21: Eastb .2E 3 (4A 20)
Swale Cl. BN24: Sto C .6A 10
Swallow Cl. BN23: Lang .3B 16
Swan Barn Bus. Cen. BN27: Hails .3F 7
Swan Barn Caravan Site BN27: Down .4F 7
Swanley Cl. BN23: Lang .3D 16
Swan Rd. BN27: Hails .3E 7
Swinburne Av. BN22: Will .2D 14
SWINGATE CROSS .2D 4
Sycamore Cl. BN22: Eastb .2F 15
Sycamore Dr. BN27: Hails .4D 6
Sycamores, The BN21: Eastb .3H 19
Sydney Rd. BN22: Eastb .1G 3 (4B 20)

T

Taddington Ho. *BN22: Eastb* .3C 20
(off Taddington Rd.)
Taddington Rd. BN22: Eastb .3C 20
Tamarack Cl. BN22: Eastb .3F 15
Tamar Cl. BN24: Sto C .6A 10
Tanbridge Rd. BN23: Lang .3F 17
Tanneries, The BN27: Mag D .3H 5
Tas Combe Way BN20: Will .3D 14
Tasmania Way BN23: Eastb .3G 17
Tavistock BN21: Eastb .4F 3
Teal Ct. BN27: Hails .2G 7
Telscombe Rd. BN23: Lang .3F 17
Tennis Cl. BN27: Hails .2D 6
Tennyson Wlk. BN23: Lang .2E 17
Tenterden Cl. BN23: Lang .3D 16
Terminus Bldgs. *BN21: Eastb* .2D 2
(off Upperton Rd.)
Terminus Pl. *BN27: Hails* .2E 7
(off Station Rd.)
Terminus Rd. BN21: Eastb .2D 2 (4H 19)
(not continuous)
Thackeray Cl. BN23: Lang .2E 17
Thatchings, The BN26: Pole .6C 8
The ....
Names prefixed with 'The' for example 'The Acorns' are indexed under the main name such as 'Acorns, The'
Thorn Lodge BN21: Eastb .4E 3
Thornton Ct. BN21: Eastb .1G 3 (4B 20)
Thornwood BN21: Eastb .1D 2 (4H 19)
Thornwood Cl. BN22: Eastb .3G 15
Thorpe, The BN20: Eastb .6C 2 (6H 19)
Thurrock Cl. BN20: Will .2C 14
Tidebrook Gdns. BN23: Lang .3F 17
(not continuous)
Tideswell Rd.
BN21: Eastb .2F 3 (4A 20)
Tilehurst Dr. BN27: Hails .1C 6
Tilgate Cl. BN21: Eastb .6F 15
Tillingham Cl. BN24: Sto C .6A 10
Tillingham Way BN24: Sto C .6A 10
Timberlaine Rd.
BN24: Pev B .5A 12
Timberley Rd. BN22: Eastb .4F 15
Timbers Ct. BN27: Hails .2E 7
Tintern Cl. BN22: Eastb .2F 15
Tolkien Rd. BN23: Lang .3F 17
Tollgate Gdns. BN23: Eastb .6D 16
Torfield Ct. BN21: Eastb .3G 19
Torfield Rd. BN21: Eastb .3G 19
Tott Yew Rd. BN20: Will .1C 14
Tourist Info. Cen.
Eastbourne .3E 3 (5A 20)
Tovey Cl. BN21: Eastb .1F 19
Tower Cl. BN24: Pev B .2D 12
Tower Mill Pl. BN26: Pole .6C 8
Towner .5E 3 (6A 20)
Trafalgar M. BN22: Eastb .3C 20
Trax Indoor Karting Cen. .5H 15
Treasure Island Adventure Pk. .3C 20
Treemaines Rd. BN23: Lang .3F 17
Triangle, The BN20: Will .2C 14
Trinity Ho. BN21: Eastb .3F 3
Trinity Pl. BN21: Eastb .3F 3 (5A 20)
Trinity Trees BN21: Eastb .3F 3 (5A 20)
Troon Cotts. BN27: Hails .1B 6
Trossachs Cl. BN23: Lang .2D 16
Trujillo Ct. BN23: Eastb .5H 17
Tudor Ct. BN21: Eastb .5D 2 (6H 19)
Tugwell Rd. BN22: Eastb .3H 15
Turnberry Dr. BN27: Hails .1C 6
Turner Cl. BN23: Lang .4D 16
Tutts Barn Ct. *BN22: Eastb* .2H 19
(off Tutts Barn La.)
Tutts Barn La. BN22: Eastb .2H 19
Tweedsmuir Cl. BN23: Lang .2C 16
Twineham Rd. BN21: Eastb .6F 15
Twitten, The *BN24: Pev B* .4B 12
(off Richmond Rd.)
Tyrone Ct. BN23: Lang .4D 16

U

Under Rd. BN27: Mag D .4H 5
Union Cl. BN27: Hails .4D 4
University of Brighton
Darley Rd. .1F 23
Hillbrow .6A 2 (6F 19)
St Anne's Rd. .3H 19
(off St Anne's Rd.)
Welkin Site .5A 2 (6G 19)
Sports Cen. .6A 2
Upland Rd. BN20: Eastb .4D 18
Upper Av.
BN21: Eastb .1E 3 & 1F 3 (3A 20)
Upper Av. Rdbt. *BN21: Eastb* .3A 20
(off Upper Av.)
Up. Carlisle Rd. BN20: Eastb .1E 23
Up. Duke's Dr. BN20: Eastb .2E 23
UPPER HORSEBRIDGE .4C 4
Up. Horsebridge Rd. BN27: Hails .4A 4
Up. King's Dr. BN20: Will .4D 14
Up. Ratton Dr. BN20: Will .5D 14
Upper St. BN20: E Dean .3B 22
UPPERTON .3G 19
Upperton Gdns. BN21: Eastb .1C 2 (4H 19)
Upperton La. BN21: Eastb .1C 2 (4H 19)
Upperton Rd. BN21: Eastb .1B 2 (3G 19)
Up. Wish Hill BN20: Will .5D 14
Upwick Rd. BN20: Eastb .4E 19
Upwyke Ho. BN21: Eastb .3E 19

V

Valentine Ct. BN21: Eastb .3E 3
Val Prinseps Rd. BN24: Pev B .5A 12
Vancouver Rd. BN23: Eastb .3H 17
Vega Cl. BN27: Hails .2F 7
Ventnor Cl. BN23: Lang .1B 16
Vernon Cl. BN23: Eastb .6E 17
Vernon Lodge BN21: Eastb .4E 3
Vian Av. BN23: Eastb .6F 17
Vicarage Dr. BN20: Eastb .4F 19
Vicarage Fld. BN27: Hails .1E 7
Vicarage La. BN20: Eastb .4F 19
BN27: Hails .1E 7
BN27: Hell .1C 4
Vicarage Rd. BN20: Eastb .1A 2 (4F 19)
BN27: Hails .2E 7
Victoria Cl. BN26: Pole .4B 8
Victoria Ct. BN21: Eastb .4F 3 (5A 20)
Victoria Dr. BN20: Eastb .1E 19
Victoria Gdns. BN20: Eastb .3D 18
Victoria Mans. BN21: Eastb .3G 3
Victoria Rd. BN20: Eastb .2D 18
BN26: Pole .4B 8
BN27: Hails .2E 7
Viking Way BN23: Eastb .5E 17
Village, The BN20: Eastb .1F 23
Village Grn. La. BN20: E Dean .3B 22
Vincent Cl. BN23: Eastb .6F 17
Vineries, The BN23: Lang .3D 16
Vine Sq. BN22: Eastb .1D 20
Vintry, The BN21: Eastb .6E 15

W

Wade Cl. BN23: Eastb .6F 17
Wadhurst Cl. BN22: Eastb .3H 15
Wakehurst Rd. BN22: Eastb .1D 20
Waldron Cl. BN22: Will .5F 15
Walford Ho. BN20: Eastb .6C 2
Walker Cl. BN23: Eastb .6F 17
Wallis Av. BN23: Eastb .6E 17
Wallis Pl. BN23: Eastb .5E 17
Wallsend Rd.
BN24: Pev, Pev B .5H 11
Walnut Tree Wlk. BN20: Will .5D 14
Walnut Wlk. BN26: Pole .5C 8
Walpole Wlk. BN23: Lang .2E 17
Walsingham Cl. BN22: Eastb .2F 15
Walton Cl. BN23: Lang .2E 17
WANNOCK .2B 14
Wannock Av. BN20: Will .1B 14
Wannock Dr. BN26: Pole .6B 8
Wannock Gdns. BN26: Pole .2B 14
Wannock La. BN20: Will .2B 14
Wannock Rd. BN22: Eastb .2D 20
BN26: Pole .1B 14
Warburton Cl. BN21: Will .5E 15
Warminster Rd. BN24: Pev B .4B 12
Warren Cl. BN20: Eastb .1E 23
BN20: Fris .2B 22
Warren Hill BN20: Eastb .6B 18
Warren La. BN20: Fris .2B 22
Warrior Ho. BN20: Eastb .1G 23
Warrior Sq. BN22: Eastb .3C 20
Wartling Rd. BN22: Eastb .1C 20
(not continuous)
BN24: Pev .2A 12
BN27: Pev, Wart .1H 11 & 2A 12
Warwick Cl. BN27: Hails .4E 5
Warwick Ct. BN23: Lang .4E 17
Waterford M. BN21: Eastb .3F 3
Waterfront, The BN23: Eastb .5G 17
Watermill Cl. BN26: Pole .6C 8
Waterworks Cotts. BN20: Fris .2A 22
Waterworks Rd. BN22: Eastb .3A 20
Watts La. BN21: Eastb .3G 19
Waverley Gdns. BN24: Pev B .4B 12

Wawmans M. *BN24: Pev B* *4B* ***12***
(off Coast Rd.)
Wayfaring Down BN26: Filch 2A **14**
Wayford Cl. BN23: Lang 3D **16**
Wayside BN20: E Dean 3B **22**
Wealden Pk. BN22: Will 4E **15**
Weatherby Cl. BN21: Will 5E **15**
Wedderburn Rd. BN20: Will 4D **14**
Welbeck Cl. BN22: Eastb 2F **15**
Wellcombe Cres. BN20: Eastb 2F **23**
Wellesley Rd.
BN21: Eastb 1F **3** (4A **20**)
Wellington Cl. BN23: Eastb 4G **17**
Wellington Ct. *BN22: Eastb* *2C* ***20***
(off Roselands Av.)
Wellington Quay BN23: Eastb 4G **17**
Wellsbourne Rd. BN24: Sto C 6A **10**
Wells Cl. BN20: Eastb 1E **23**
Wellsmead Pk. BN20: Eastb 1F **23**
Wenthill Cl. BN20: E Dean 2B **22**
Went Hill Gdns. BN22: Will 2D **14**
Went La. BN20: E Dean 2C **22**
Went Way BN20: E Dean 3B **22**
Wentworth Cl. BN27: Hails 6B **4**
Wentworth Ct. BN23: Eastb 1E **21**
Wesley Pl. *BN22: Eastb* *2C* ***20***
(off Ringwood Rd.)
Wessex Pl. *BN20: Eastb* *2E* ***19***
(off Victoria Dr.)
Westcliffe Ct. BN20: Eastb 6D **2**
Westcliff Mansion BN20: Eastb 6D **2**
West Cl. BN26: Pole 4D **8**
Westdown Ho. BN21: Eastb 3F **3**
Westerham Rd. BN23: Lang 4D **16**
Western Av. BN26: Pole 5D **8**
Western Pde. BN20: Eastb 6E **3** (2H **23**)
BN21: Eastb 6E **3** (2H **23**)
Western Rd. BN22: Eastb 3B **20**
BN24: Pev B 5B **12**
BN27: Hails 1C **6**
Westfield Cl. BN26: Pole 4C **8**
Westfield Ct. BN26: Pole 4C **8**
Westfield Rd. BN21: Eastb 1F **19**
WESTHAM 5F **11**
Westham Bus. Pk. BN24: W'ham 1F **17**
Westham Dr. BN24: Pev B 3D **12**
West House BN21: Eastb 4E **3** (5A **20**)
Westlords BN20: Will 5E **15**
Westminster Cl. BN22: Eastb 1F **15**
Westmorland Ct. BN20: Eastb 6D **14**
West St. BN21: Eastb 3D **2** (5H **19**)
West St. M. BN21: Eastb 3D **2**
West Ter. BN21: Eastb 2D **2** (5H **19**)
Wexford Ct. *BN23: Lang* *4D* ***16***
(off Biddenden Cl.)
Wharf Rd. BN21: Eastb 2D **2** (4H **19**)
Wheelwright Cl. BN22: Eastb 1F **15**
Whiffens Cl. BN27: Hails 3C **6**
Whitbread Cl. BN23: Lang 1B **16**
WHITE DYKE 3H **7**
White Dyke Rd. BN27: Hails 3G **7**
White Gables BN21: Eastb 5D **2** (6H **19**)
Whitehill Cl. BN20: Eastb 2D **18**
Whitley Cl. BN22: Eastb 2C **20**
Whitley Rd. BN22: Eastb 3A **20**
Whittle Dr. BN23: Eastb 4A **16**
Wicklow Ct. *BN23: Lang* *4D* ***16***
(off Biddenden Cl.)
Wildwood BN23: Lang 1C **16**
Willard Cl. BN22: Eastb 1A **20**
Williams Ct. BN23: Lang 4E **17**
WILLINGDON 4D **14**
Willingdon Cl. BN20: Will 4D **14**
Willingdon Ct. BN20: Will 2C **14**
Willingdon Drove
BN23: Eastb, Lang 4A **16**
Willingdon Golf Course 6D **14**
Willingdon Pk. Dr. BN22: Eastb, Will 3E **15**
Willingdon Rd. BN20: Eastb, Will 4E **15**
BN21: Eastb 5E **15**
Willingdon Rdbt. BN20: Will 5E **15**
Willingdon Way BN22: Will 3D **14**
Willoughby Cres. BN22: Eastb 1C **20**
Willow Av. BN27: Hails 6D **4**
Willow Ct. *BN26: Pole* *5C* ***8***
(off Walnut Wlk.)
Willowdowne Cl. BN26: Pole 6C **8**
Willow Dr. BN26: Pole 6C **8**
Willowfield Rd. BN22: Eastb 1H **3** (4B **20**)
Willowfield Sq. BN22: Eastb 1H **3** (4B **20**)
Willows, The BN27: Hails 4C **4**
Willow Wlk. BN22: Eastb 3F **15**
Wilmington Gdns.
BN21: Eastb 5E **3** (6A **20**)
Wilmington Sq.
BN21: Eastb 5E **3** (6A **20**)
Wilton Av. BN22: Eastb 2H **15**
Wiltshire Ct. BN23: Lang 4E **17**
Winchcombe Rd.
BN22: Eastb 1F **3** (3A **20**)
Winchelsea Rd. BN22: Eastb 1D **20**
Winchester Ho. BN22: Eastb 2G **15**
Winchester Way BN22: Will 3D **14**
Windermere Ct. BN21: Eastb 3F **3**
Windermere Cres. BN22: Eastb 2C **20**
Windmill Cl. BN21: Eastb 1F **19**
Windmill Grn. BN24: Sto C 6B **10**
Windmill La. BN20: Fris 2A **22**
Windmill Pl. BN26: Pole 6C **8**
Windmill Rd. BN26: Pole 6C **8**
Windover Way BN22: Will 2D **14**
Windsor Cl. BN23: Lang 2C **16**
Windsor Ct. BN22: Eastb 1H **3** (4B **20**)
BN26: Pole 4C **8**
Windsor Rd. BN27: Hails 3D **6**
Windsor Way BN26: Pole 4C **8**
Windward Quay BN23: Eastb 5F **17**
Winkney Rd. BN22: Eastb 2H **15**
Winston Cres. BN23: Eastb 6D **16**
Winter Garden Theatre 5E **3** (6A **20**)
Wish Hill BN20: Will 4D **14**
Wish Rd. BN21: Eastb 3E **3** (5A **20**)
Withyham Cl. BN22: Eastb 4H **15**
Woburn Cl. BN27: Hails 6C **4**
Woburn Way BN22: Eastb 2F **15**
Woodcroft Dr. BN21: Will 6E **15**
Woodgate Rd. BN22: Eastb 2B **20**
Woodland Av. BN22: Will 5E **15**
Woodlands Cl. BN27: Hails 5E **5**
Woodland Vale Cotts. *BN26: Pole* *6B* ***8***
(off Wannock Rd.)
Woodpecker Dr. BN27: Hails 1C **6**
Woodpecker Rd. BN23: Lang 3B **16**
Woodside Way BN27: Hails 5C **6**
Woodward Cl. BN23: Eastb 6E **17**
Wordsworth Dr. BN23: Lang 3E **17**
Wrestwood Av. BN22: Will 4E **15**
Wrotham Cl. BN23: Lang 4D **16**
Wroxham Rd. BN23: Lang 1B **16**

Y

Yews, The BN21: Eastb 1E **3**
Yew Tree Ct. *BN21: Eastb* *3F* ***3***
(off Trinity Trees)
Yieldings Cl. BN21: Eastb 2F **19**
York Rd. BN21: Eastb 3D **2** (5H **19**)
Yorkshire Ct. BN20: Eastb 6D **14**
Youl Grange BN20: Eastb 6F **19**

The representation on the maps of a road, track or footpath is no evidence of the existence of a right of way.

The Grid on this map is the National Grid taken from Ordnance Survey® mapping with the permission of the Controller of Her Majesty's Stationery Office.

SAFETY CAMERA INFORMATION

PocketGPSWorld.com's CamerAlert is a self-contained speed and red light camera warning system for SatNavs and Android or Apple iOS smartphones/tablets. Visit www.cameralert.co.uk to download.

Safety camera locations are publicised by the Safer Roads Partnership which operates them in order to encourage drivers to comply with speed limits at these sites. It is the driver's absolute responsibility to be aware of and to adhere to speed limits at all times.

By showing this safety camera information it is the intention of Geographers' A-Z Map Company Ltd., to encourage safe driving and greater awareness of speed limits and vehicle speed. Data accurate at time of printing.